GARY NULL'S POWER FOODS

GARY NULL'S

POWER
FOODS

The 15 Best Foods for Your Health

Gary Null, Ph.D.

 NEW AMERICAN LIBRARY

New American Library
Published by New American Library, a division of
Penguin Group (USA) Inc., 375 Hudson Street,
New York, New York 10014, USA
Penguin Group (Canada), 90 Eglinton Avenue East, Suite 700, Toronto,
Ontario M4P 2Y3, Canada (a division of Pearson Penguin Canada Inc.)
Penguin Books Ltd., 80 Strand, London WC2R 0RL, England
Penguin Ireland, 25 St. Stephen's Green, Dublin 2,
Ireland (a division of Penguin Books Ltd.)
Penguin Group (Australia), 250 Camberwell Road, Camberwell, Victoria 3124,
Australia (a division of Pearson Australia Group Pty. Ltd.)
Penguin Books India Pvt. Ltd., 11 Community Centre, Panchsheel Park,
New Delhi - 110 017, India
Penguin Group (NZ), cnr Airborne and Rosedale Roads, Albany,
Auckland 1310, New Zealand (a division of Pearson New Zealand Ltd.)
Penguin Books (South Africa) (Pty.) Ltd., 24 Sturdee Avenue,
Rosebank, Johannesburg 2196, South Africa

Penguin Books Ltd., Registered Offices:
80 Strand, London WC2R 0RL, England

First published by New American Library,
a division of Penguin Group (USA) Inc.

Copyright © Gary Null & Associates, Inc., 2006
All rights reserved

 REGISTERED TRADEMARK — MARCA REGISTRADA

ISBN-13: 978-0-451-21976-3

Designed by Patrice Sheriden

Printed in the United States of America

PUBLISHER'S NOTE

Every effort has been made to ensure that the information contained in this book is complete and accurate. However, neither the publisher nor the author is engaged in rendering professional advice or services to the individual reader. The ideas, procedures, and suggestions contained in this book are not intended as a substitute for consulting with your physician. All matters regarding your health require medical supervision. Neither the author nor the publisher shall be liable or responsible for any loss or damage allegedly arising from any information or suggestion in this book. The opinions expressed in this book represent the personal views of the author and not of the publisher.

The recipes contained in this book are to be followed exactly as written. The publisher is not responsible for your specific health or allergy needs that may require medical supervision. The publisher is not responsible for any adverse reactions to the recipes contained in this book. The publisher does not have any control over and does not assume any responsibility for author or third-party Web sites or their content.

This book is dedicated to
everyone who loves to eat,
but hates to cook.

ACKNOWLEDGMENTS

Creating, testing, and documenting more than three hundred original recipes is a tasty, but tremendous undertaking. I am most grateful to all those who shopped for, prepared, presented, photographed, taste-tested, and faithfully recorded each of these recipes.

From Florida to New York, I am grateful to the top-notch team who assisted me in creating this cookbook. Special thanks to my daughter and chef extraordinaire, Shelly Null, and to Manette Loudon and Jeanette Emmarco, for editorial assistance. In the Florida Kitchen, thanks to Roxanne Begin, Claire Adams, Christina Stevens, Doreen Starling, Bryan Hantman, Lydia Semczyszyn, and Linda Gluck. I am grateful for the culinary skills of the talented chefs at Gary Null's Uptown Whole Foods in New York: Nazmul Khandaker, Asirrudin Ahmed, Edgar Duran, Mizael Vasquez, Felipe Montealegre, Guadelpe Cortez, Mohammad Hossain, and Serafin Gonzalez. Thanks also to Mercedes Trinidad, Jody Blanchard, Jesse Hunter, and Robert Silverstein, for their efforts. Finally, my thanks to Melissa Goldman, Dan Demetriad, Meri Wayne, and Jay Graygor, for making each of the dishes in this book look as good as they taste.

CONTENTS

SECTION 1

INTRODUCTION

For my entire career—more than thirty years—I have been preaching about the relationship between diet and mental and physical health. There is a direct correlation between what we eat and our bodies' and brains' resilience, vitality, and response to everyday stress and aging. This simple fact has been proven by scientific studies and affirmed by countless experts in the fields of nutrition, medicine, and mental health.

It seems so basic, doesn't it? Eat well for best health—and it's increasingly convenient to do so. Most supermarkets have organic produce and natural foods sections, and there are specialty shops, publications, and Web sites catering to those who seek to pursue the healthiest diet and optimal nutrition. Yet the average American's diet is unhealthy, filled with processed, denatured foods that are excessively high in protein and saturated fats. When I look around me I am dismayed to see the number of Americans who are overweight yet poorly nourished, whose bodies are unable to resist everyday stresses, and a range of diseases from cancer to diabetes, to heart disease, to conditions that cause devastating physical or mental impairment, such as Parkinson's or Alzheimer's. And I cannot sit quietly and allow people to compromise their health and their futures. Not when, with a little education, changes in diet and a focus on optimal nutrition can result in vast improvements in our mental and physical welfare.

I'm sympathetic to those of you who argue that you have tried "health foods" and found them lacking in texture and taste. But having eaten a vegan diet for more than thirty years, I know firsthand that food that is good for you does not have to taste bland. Furthermore, a diet that is meat- and dairy-free offers a wide range of health and environmental benefits: respect for the life of the animal, protection of the environment, better use of sustainable agriculture, and protection from diseases linked to consuming animal products.

In earlier books, I have recommended recipes using dairy, albeit organic, natural dairy, and without hormones, and have included recipes featuring fish because of scientific literature about the importance of omega-3 fatty acids. In this book I want to show you how you can enjoy all the health benefits and variety and good tastes of a strictly plant-based diet.

And the good news is that more Americans are becoming aware of meatless choices. Adults, teenagers, and even children have eliminated meat from their diets. Many restaurants and caterers now routinely offer vegetarian choices.

But simply choosing to become a "vegetarian" isn't enough to ensure optimal health. People may choose to eat a meat-free diet because they oppose animal suffering. These same people, however, who claim to participate in a healthy nutritional lifestyle may fill up on pizza, white bread, or refined sugars. They may smoke, drink, and have sedentary lifestyles. Even people who follow vegan or raw foods diets may be lacking in important nutrients such as B_{12}, acetyl-L-carnitine, and L-carnosine. Planning a vegetarian or vegan diet doesn't have to be complicated, but it is important to ensure that you consume a wide variety of foods in order to meet all your body's nutrient needs. It is worth it to take some time to educate yourself about optimal nutrition and health by reading my publication *Seven Steps to Perfect Health*, visiting my Web site, www.garynull.com, or reading my other books and articles on nutrition and a healthy lifestyle.

Many of my books include many recipes that offer healthy eating options that can help in the treatment of certain conditions and generally promote optimal health. Here, for the first time, I have collected more than three hundred new recipes in one book, to allow you to enjoy a rich and varied eating plan that ensures you make the healthiest choices for your daily meals.

What is truly exciting about this book is that I have based the recipes around a core of fifteen "Power Foods"—foods that are packed with nutrients and disease-fighting properties. These fifteen foods are easy to find and lend themselves to incredibly tasty and easy-to-prepare dishes. When combined with a wide range of other natural, healthy foods, these Power Foods ensure that you are giving your body exactly what it needs for optimum vitality and health at every meal.

The recipes in this book are all meat-, dairy-, and wheat-free. Consequently, those who are allergic or gluten-intolerant can enjoy every dish. I have also incorporated a number of raw dishes. Those who are aware of the benefits of raw foods will notice that many dishes are prepared to specifically retain the highest levels of beneficial enzymes, phytonutrients, phytosterols, chlorophyll, and antioxidants of the ingredients in their natural states.

In this cookbook I prove that healthy foods don't have to be boring foods. Each nutrition-packed recipe in this book is not only good for you but is also appealing to the senses. Whether you are making a meal for yourself, for your family, or for entertaining, the soups, salads, desserts, entrées, and side dishes in this book are all quick and easy to prepare. The recipes have all been tested with my chefs in my gourmet kitchen, including my daughter Shelly, who is a gourmet chef in my health food store in New York City. The juices were all tested with regular customers at my juice bar in Gary Null's Uptown Whole Foods, where they gave their feedback. These recipes rely on natural flavorings and can easily be altered to accommodate your own particular taste. If you prefer a spicy dish, experiment with adding more heat. If you prefer a milder flavor, reduce the spices used. The ingredients in these dishes lend themselves perfectly to experimentation, and I encourage you to become a creative chef.

In the next chapter I will explain how to use this book to get the most daily benefit from my Power Foods. Chapter Two lists each of the Power Foods and their incredible nutritional and health benefits. After that you can browse through hundreds of recipes for Beverages, Breakfast Dishes, Appetizers and Dips, Soups, Salads, Side Dishes, Entrées, and Desserts. Finally, I provide two weeks' worth of meal plans that allow you to sample a wide variety of dishes while providing your body with the ultimate in nutritional benefits.

I hope you use this unique cookbook to create a lifetime diet plan that enhances both your experience of eating and your overall health. I encourage you to share these flavorful, nutrient-rich dishes with friends and family and introduce others to the delicious benefits of my Power Foods recipes.

Chapter One

HOW TO USE
THIS COOKBOOK

This cookbook is more than simply a collection of mouthwatering recipes. It contains critical ingredients for a lifetime of good health. By following a nutritional plan that is simple, nonrestrictive, and nutrient-dense, you will gain energy, focus, and mental and physical vitality. Proper nutrition is essential in creating, protecting, and restoring good health. Each of the fifteen Power Foods used in this book has a specific, positive influence on your overall health and well-being. While it is important to include a wide range of foods in your diet, I have highlighted these fifteen foods in particular because they offer tremendous nutritional value, particularly when used in the combinations in the recipes that follow. In addition to being loaded with beneficial vitamins, minerals, and antioxidants, all of these foods lend themselves to an extensive variety of uses in the kitchen. In addition to their remarkable nutritional values, these Power Foods are powerfully versatile.

You can quickly refer to the nutritional value of any recipe in this book by noting its Power Food designation. A recipe designated "Power 1" contains one of the fifteen Power Foods; the designation "Power 2" means the recipe calls for two of the featured foods, and so on. You should strive to incorporate as many of the Power Foods as you can into your daily diet, while enjoying a wide variety of the other nutrient-rich foods used as ingredients in the dishes in this book.

While you can create a healthy eating plan by simply choosing daily from the recipes offered in this book, it is important to take the time to understand the fundamental effect of proper nutrition on our bodies. In the next chapter, I will discuss the specific benefits of each of the Power Foods, but there are also some important general rules to follow in creating a plan for eating your way to optimal health. Keep the following information in mind when choosing the ingredients that will make up your daily meals.

Complex carbohydrates provide your body with fiber necessary for good health and digestion. They help in lowering cholesterol and blood pressure levels. A diet rich in fiber may help prevent or alleviate conditions such as constipation, colon and rectal cancer, heart disease, breast cancer, diabetes, and obesity. Carbohydrates also break down into glucose, which is an important energy source for the body and brain. Complex carbohydrates should be eaten in whole food form. Grain foods, such as oats, rice, rye, whole wheat, millet, corn, or quinoa, can be found in cereal, breads, and pastas. Beans are also an excellent source of complex carbohydrates and fiber.

Fruits and vegetables are packed with essential vitamins and protective antioxidants that promote best health. Antioxidants, which work to protect the cells against damaging free radicals in the body, are naturally occurring in many fruits and vegetables. Eating these beneficial foods helps to detoxify the body, ridding it of free radicals. Richly colored fruits and vegetables, such as blueberries, kale, spinach, and cherries, have the highest levels of antioxidants.

All the fruits and vegetables you eat should be organic, whenever possible. It is now much easier to obtain fresh organic produce in your local grocery store, and there are frozen varieties available, which will do in a pinch. In many of the recipes, fruits and vegetables are used with their skins on, since the skins and peels contain valuable nutrients. If you are buying conventional fruits or vegetables, wash them well, with a pesticide-reducing wash. You may also wish to peel or remove skins from conventionally grown fruits and vegetables before juicing because the skin harbors most of the pesticide residue.

Protein is an important nutritional building block. Our bodies use protein to build and repair tissues, and make enzymes, hormones, and other body chemicals. Protein is not stored in the body, however, so it is important to consume the correct amounts of high-quality protein daily. Most adults require 40 to 70 grams of protein per day depending on their size, physical activity, and state of health. It may be more or less depending on the uniqueness of their lifestyles. This protein should not be animal protein. The best foods for high-quality protein are grains (such as buckwheat, brown rice, spelt, rye, and oats), legumes, nuts, seeds, tofu, tempeh, yams, sweet potatoes, squashes, and cruciferous vegetables. Soy and rice protein powders are also protein sources, and can easily be mixed into smoothies for a protein-rich, drinkable meal.

Fats are essential for the functioning of both body and brain. They also play an important role in many recipes, enhancing flavors and textures. It is critically important to choose the right kinds of fats, however. The saturated fats and trans fats found in processed foods, such as commercial salad dressings, margarines, boxed cakes, microwave popcorn, and fast foods, should be avoided at all costs. Excess saturated fat has been linked to an increased likelihood of cardiovascular disease and high LDL ("bad") cholesterol. But there are good fats that should be included in our daily diets. One of the best ways to incorporate healthy fats into your diet is by choosing to eat nuts and seeds (such as almonds, walnuts, and pine nuts, and pumpkin, sunflower, flax, and sesame seeds) and to use olive, sesame, or coconut oils in recipes.

Basic Rules for Good Nutrition

The recipes in this cookbook make it easy to follow my basic rules for good nutrition with dishes that look appealing and don't sacrifice taste or variety. Creating daily meal plans from these recipes makes it effortless to follow my twelve basic nutritional rules for good eating habits:

- Avoid meat and shellfish.
- Avoid dairy, including milk, yogurt, cheese, butter, ice cream,

or cream sauces. Replace these items with rice milk, nut milk, or soymilk and foods made from nondairy substitutes. Avoid any nondairy substitute made with casein.

- Avoid caffeine and alcohol.
- Avoid sugar and artificial sweeteners. Replace them with stevia, agave, molasses, maple syrup, and honey.
- Avoid deep-fried or processed foods.
- Avoid food additives, preservatives, color or flavoring agents, and MSG.
- Eat organic products.
- Eat nuts and nut butters.
- Eat soybeans and soy products.
- Eat whole grains (such as quinoa, amaranth, and spelt).
- Eat legumes (such as lentils, lima beans, black beans, and garbanzo beans).
- Drink plenty of water.

A Note About Raw Foods

All of the recipes in this cookbook are created for vegans and vegetarians. But a number of recipes in this book are also suitable for those who follow a raw foods diet. Generally speaking, a "raw food" is one that has not been altered by any method that would change its basic chemical structure through heating over 118°F. Raw foods do not contain any chemical preservatives. The idea of eating raw foods has been prominent since the twentieth century, with proponents advocating the use of sprouts, seeds, and fresh vegetable juices in preparing meals. As you know, I have always advocated for the benefits of such foods, and have made it my mission to promote the clear link between optimal health and nutrition and the benefits of juicing and raw foods.

As you look through this cookbook, you will notice that the raw foods dishes are simple and easy to prepare. They can be eaten immediately to allow you to enjoy the purest, unaltered tastes of the foods used to create them.

A Note About Supplements

Individuals following a vegan or vegetarian diet that is widely inclusive of all food groups generally consume most of the nutrients needed for optimal health. I do believe, however, that supplements can further enhance the natural nutrients present in fresh foods. Rather than take many separate supplements, I suggest daily multisupplements, such as my Gary Null AM/PM formulations (available at my Web site, www.garynull.com).

Be Inspired

This cookbook raises the bar for vegan and vegetarian cuisine. Nearly all the recipes contain one or more of the Power Foods I've identified as having optimal benefits and maximum versatility in preparing delicious dishes. To get you started, I've also included fourteen days of menu selections. Follow a specific menu or mix in your favorites from any category. Eating for best health does not need to be boring or bland. Feel free to experiment with seasonings, substitutions, and different food combinations to tailor dishes to your specific tastes. Most recipes make between one and four servings. It is easy to increase the serving size of any of the recipes. You may find that you prefer making large quantities of your favorite dishes and enjoying them over a few days' time. Please note, however, that most of the juices and raw dishes should be enjoyed immediately after preparation and will not retain their nutritional value—or good taste—if stored.

I am happy to be able to offer such an extensive collection of healthy, nutritious recipes in one easy-to-use cookbook. I encourage you to make this cookbook your daily resource for meal preparation so you may enjoy all the benefits the Power Foods offer: taste, nutrition, and optimum health!

Chapter Two

THE POWER FOODS

Each of the fifteen foods that follow in the list below is featured in nearly every recipe in this cookbook. They were chosen because of their proven health benefits and their versatility in creating flavorful dishes. Enjoying all of these foods daily is an important part of a diet that will enhance your health, vitality, and mental vigor. In this chapter, I will explain the specific nutritional qualities of each of the Power Foods.

The Fifteen Power Foods

Almonds
Oranges
Bananas
Blueberries
Onions
Garlic
Ginger
Legumes
Carrots

Peppers
Shiitake Mushrooms
Tomatoes
Leafy Greens
Soy
Whole Grains

Benefits of Power Foods

Almonds

Almonds are tasty and versatile. They are delicious as a plain snack and add a delicate flavor to recipes. They are packed with protein; a quarter cup contains 7.55 grams, over 15% of the recommended daily protein allowance. Almonds are also high in monounsaturated fats, the "good" fat that is linked to a reduced risk of cardiovascular disease. Studies have shown that substituting almonds for other foods high in saturated fats has a positive effect in reducing blood levels of LDL ("bad") cholesterol. Other studies suggest that almonds may play a role in promoting colon health and preventing gallstones.

The meat of almonds is high in vitamin E, and over twenty potent antioxidant flavonoids have been found in almond skins. A one-quarter-cup serving of almonds contains only 213 calories and is an excellent source of magnesium, protein, fiber, potassium, calcium, phosphorus, and iron. It provides about 40% of the RDV (recommended daily value) for vitamin E; 18% of the RDV for vitamin B_2 (riboflavin); and nearly 4.5 grams of fiber.

Furthermore, magnesium acts as a calcium channel blocker, allowing veins and arteries to relax, thus improving blood flow and improving blood pressure and arterial health. Potassium is an electrolyte involved in neural transmission and is essential for maintaining heart function. Almonds are also a good source for the trace minerals manganese and copper, two important antioxidants that are essential cofactors of a key oxidative enzyme called superoxide dismutase. Superoxide dismutase scavenges damaging free radicals and converts them into hydrogen peroxide and oxygen.

Oranges

High in vitamin C and dietary fiber, oranges add a sweet citrus flavor to many dishes. Like blueberries, the orange's vibrant color is indicative of the powerful antioxidants that make this juicy fruit a popular choice in healthy diets.

One orange contains only 62 calories and is packed with vitamin C (116% RDV), fiber (over 3 grams), folate (nearly 10% RDV), and significant amounts of vitamin B_1 (thiamin), potassium, vitamin A, and calcium.

While oranges are loaded with antioxidants, it is the hesperidin flavonoid that has been getting attention lately for its strong anti-inflammatory properties. Besides acting to promote healthy blood vessel function, hesperidin is also beneficial in reducing cholesterol. Most of this phytonutrient is found in the peel of the orange. Always purchase organic oranges so you can derive the most benefit from this powerful phytonutrient by juicing the oranges with their peels and incorporating orange zest into recipes.

The vitamin C found in oranges is an important antioxidant. A good intake of vitamin C is associated with immunity support and a reduced risk of colon cancer. Vitamin C reduces damaging free radicals and reduces oxidative stress that can cause arterial plaque buildup or high cholesterol.

A 2003 Australian study notes positive effects associated with citrus consumption for conditions ranging from arthritis to diabetes, to impaired lung function, to Alzheimer's, Parkinson's, and Crohn's diseases (CSIRO, "The Health Benefits of Citrus Fruits," December 2003).

The pulp of the orange is also an excellent source of fiber. The naturally occurring sugar in oranges (fructose) helps to keep blood sugar levels under control.

Like carrots, oranges contain carotenoids, natural fat-soluble pigments found in certain plants that provide their bright coloration and serve as antioxidants and a source for vitamin A activity. These carotenoids are associated with protection from heart disease and cancer, improved night vision, and improved blood sugar regulation. Research also suggests that vitamin A may reduce the risk of emphysema, even among smokers or those who are exposed to secondhand smoke.

Oranges can be stored for up to two weeks, either at room temperature or in the refrigerator. After two weeks, however, they begin to lose vitamin content. So enjoy oranges frequently—and not just for breakfast!

Bananas

Bananas may be nature's most perfect snack food. They're neatly packaged, available year-round, and have a sweet taste that makes them a great substitute for sugary treats. But bananas are much more than a smart addition to the lunch box. At just over 100 calories, a banana packs a powerful nutritional punch, providing 34% of the RDV of vitamin B_6, nearly 18% of the RDV of vitamin C, 13% of the RDV of potassium, nearly 3 grams of dietary fiber, and 9% of the RDV of manganese.

A lack of vitamin B_6 in the diet has been linked to insomnia, weakness, and irritability. Potassium is an electrolyte involved in neural transmission and is essential for maintaining heart function. Bananas are a good source of pectin, a soluble fiber that absorbs fluid, helping to normalize movement through the digestive tract and improve nutrient absorption. Bananas are also rich in a probiotic compound called fructooligosaccharide that may specifically aid in calcium absorption by stimulating the production of probiotic bacteria in the colon. Increased probiotic bacteria also help protect our bodies against harmful microorganisms that can cause digestive problems and other ailments. Bananas are also a good source of starch, which converts to complex carbohydrates for slow-burning energy production.

The results of a 2005 study published in the *International Journal of Cancer* suggest that bananas may offer protection against kidney cancer. While an increased consumption of whole fruits and vegetables can cut kidney cancer risk in half, women who ate bananas four to six times a week halved their risk of developing the disease, compared to those who did not eat the fruit.

Blueberries

Blueberries are packed full of nutrients and are one of the most potent antioxidant fruits you can eat. Their flavor ranges from tart to sweet, making them a versatile ingredient in recipes both savory and sweet.

A cup of blueberries has about 80 calories and provides 31% of the RDV of vitamin C, 20% of the RDV of manganese, nearly 4 grams of dietary fiber, and over 7% of the RDV for vitamin E.

One of the most exciting nutritional properties of blueberries is their abundance of antioxidants called anthocyanidins. These powerful phytonutrients neutralize free radical damage that affects the collagen matrix of cells and tissues. Anthocyanidins are the blue-red pigments found in blueberries and are credited with enhancing the effects of vitamin C, enhancing the health of all body tissues, protecting the cardiovascular system, protecting the brain from oxidative stress, and improving brain function by crossing the blood-brain barrier to localize in the brain regions controlling spatial learning and memory. Studies have shown that people who eat a cup of blueberries each day perform well on tests of motor skills.

Another powerful antioxidant found in blueberries, pterostilebene, is already acknowledged as a heart-disease-fighting and cancer-fighting phytonutrient, but new studies show that it may also help lower cholesterol. Another antioxidant compound, ellagic acid, may help block the metabolic pathways that can lead to cancer.

Blueberries are also high in pectin, a soluble fiber that absorbs fluid, helping to normalize movement through the digestive tract and improve nutrient absorption. Rapid movement of waste through the digestive system may be a factor in reducing the risk of colon cancers. Blueberries also contain tannins, which act as anti-inflammatories in the digestive system. Researchers at Rutgers University have also identified a compound in blueberries that promotes urinary tract health, reducing the risk of infection by preventing E. coli bacteria from adhering to the cells lining the walls of the urinary tract.

Onions

The strong aroma of an onion isn't the only powerful thing about this layered bulb. Onions, like garlic, are rich in powerful sulfur-containing compounds that have a host of healthy properties. In general, the more pungent the onion, the greater the health benefits, although shallots and scallions share the health-enhancing benefits of the more commonly used yellow onions.

Onions are rich in chromium, a trace mineral that helps cells respond to insulin. One cup of raw onions contains 20% of the RDV for chromium, as well as high levels of vitamin C (17% RDV), fiber (nearly 3 grams), manganese (11% RDV), molybdenum (a trace mineral that plays a role in three enzyme systems involved in the metabolism of carbohydrates, fats, and proteins, and is also found in tooth enamel; 10% RDV), and significant amounts of vitamin B$_6$, tryptophan, folate, potassium, phosphorous, and copper.

Studies have found that high onion consumption lowers blood sugar levels, decreases total cholesterol, and increases levels of HDL ("good") cholesterol. Onions are high in chromium, a trace mineral that is depleted by consuming refined sugars and white flour products. Not surprisingly, marginal chromium deficiency is not uncommon among Americans.

Because onion helps lower blood pressure, lower cholesterol, and promote good, HDL cholesterol, it is beneficial in preventing conditions such as heart disease or stroke. The B$_6$ found in onions also lowers homocysteine levels, another factor in preventing heart attack and stroke.

The results of a study published in the March 2005 *Journal of Agriculture and Food Chemistry* suggest that onions may boost bone health as well. A compound known as GPCS may inhibit the action of the cells that break down bone.

Like garlic, onion boasts anti-inflammatory, antibacterial benefits and may be helpful in reducing the inflammation associated with conditions such as asthma, arthritis, and respiratory congestion accompanying the common cold. A potent flavonoid called quercetin works with the vitamin C in onions to help kill harmful bacteria, perhaps helping to prevent you from coming down with that cold in the first place.

Garlic

Garlic is an essential ingredient for cooks all over the world. Available in fresh, dried, or powdered form, it is simple to find, easy to use, and offers an array of health benefits that truly earn it the designation as a "Power Food." Fresh garlic offers the most nutritional benefit and should be used as often as possible. Whole garlic bulbs will keep fresh from two weeks to two months. Once you break the head of garlic, its shelf life is reduced to just a few days, so enjoy it freely.

Garlic is rich in a variety of powerful sulfur-containing compounds and is an excellent source of other important nutrients. One ounce of garlic provides manganese (23% RDV), vitamin B_6 (over 17% RDV), and vitamin C (nearly 15% RDV). It also provides tryptophan, selenium, calcium, phosphorus, vitamin B_1 (thiamin), copper, and even a small amount of protein (almost 2 grams).

The health benefits of garlic are extensive. Numerous studies have demonstrated its properties in protection from heart disease and stroke. Garlic inhibits cardiac artery calcification and lessens the amounts of free radicals in the bloodstream, contributing to the reduction of plaque deposits in the arteries. Regular consumption of garlic also lowers blood pressure and decreases LDL ("bad") cholesterol levels in the blood.

The vitamin C in garlic is a first-line antioxidant defender in the bloodstream, and the vitamin B_6 helps lower levels of homocysteine, an enzyme that can damage cell walls. Selenium protects against cancer and heavy metals toxicity, and manganese is an essential cofactor of the key oxidative enzyme superoxide dismutase, which scavenges damaging free radicals and converts them into hydrogen peroxide and oxygen.

Garlic also contains anti-inflammatory compounds that aid in protection from conditions like asthma and arthritis. It also contains antiviral and antibacterial compounds that fight harmful microbes that can cause common infections like colds, stomach viruses, and yeast infections. The results of a July 2003 study published in the *Archives of Dermatological Research* suggest that an organosulfur compound found in garlic may be useful in the treatment of skin cancer, and other studies have shown that consumption of garlic may play a role in the prevention of colon cancer.

Ginger

Ginger's spicy taste adds a zest to many dishes and is particularly recognizable in Asian dishes. Fresh ginger is preferable to the dried form found in the spice section of supermarkets. Fresh ginger can be stored, unpeeled, in the freezer for up to six months, and in the refrigerator (unpeeled) for up to three weeks. The tough outer skin should be peeled before using fresh ginger.

In herbal medicine, ginger is recognized for its ability to soothe and protect the intestinal tract, and it has long been used to treat symptoms of gastrointestinal distress. Ginger is also a potent antioxidant and offers anti-inflammatory effects. Ginger's spicy taste may also help to promote healthy detoxification through sweating.

One ounce of ginger offers significant amounts of potassium, magnesium, copper, manganese, and vitamin B_6. It is credited with alleviating the symptoms of motion sickness, and nausea during pregnancy. Ginger also contains gingerols, potent anti-inflammatory compounds that may help to improve mobility and reduce pain in patients with arthritis. Gingerols may also provide some protection against colorectal cancer, according to research presented in a 2003 meeting of cancer experts (Frontiers in Cancer Prevention Research, in Phoenix, Arizona).

Legumes

Legumes are an excellent source of cholesterol-lowering fiber and energy-boosting protein and iron. No one bean has an advantage over the others in providing important nutrients, so all beans may be considered as Power Foods, and I have tried to create recipes using a broad sampling of legumes to allow you to take advantage of all the benefits offered by this food group.

For instance, lentils may be small, but their high fiber content is important in managing blood sugar, as it prevents blood sugar levels from rising too rapidly after a meal. One cup of cooked lentils provides 63% of the RDV of dietary fiber, as well as significant amounts of heart-healthy nutrients such as folate (90% RDV) and magnesium (18% RDV), and lentils provide 36% of the RDV for hemoglobin-supporting iron.

Black beans are rich in anthocyanidins, a potent antioxidant credited with enhancing the effects of vitamin C, enhancing the health of all body tissues, protecting the cardiovascular system, protecting the brain from oxidative stress, and improving brain function by crossing the blood-brain barrier to localize in the brain regions controlling spatial learning and memory. One cup of black beans can provide 30% of your RDV of protein.

Kidney beans provide 18% of the RDV of B_1 (thiamin), a vitamin necessary for the synthesis of acetylcholine, an important neurotransmitter essential for memory.

Green beans are rich in vitamin K (122% RDV), which is necessary for bone support. They are also a good source of vitamin C (20% RDV).

One cup of garbanzo beans provides high amounts of molybdenum (a trace mineral that plays a role in three enzyme systems involved in the metabolism of carbohydrates, fats, and proteins, and is also found in tooth enamel; 164% RDV), as well as manganese (85% RDV), folate (70% RDV), and tryptophan (44% RDV). Garbanzo beans are also a great source of trace minerals such as copper and phosphorus.

Fiber-rich legumes play an important role in the prevention of gallstones, increased cardiac health, regulation of blood sugar, lowered cholesterol (and increased good, HDL cholesterol) levels, and protection from cancers, especially colorectal cancer.

Carrots

The bright orange color of carrots is your first clue that this sweet, crunchy vegetable is packed with protective, disease-fighting antioxidant compounds. What may surprise you is just how many nutrients are packed into this modest root vegetable.

One cup of raw carrots has just 53 calories and provides an astounding 683% of the RDV of vitamin A, 221% of the RDV of vitamin K, 19% of the RDV for vitamin C, nearly 4 grams of dietary fiber, 11% of the RDV of potassium, 9% of the RDV for vitamin B_6, over 8% of the RDV of manganese, 8% of the RDV of vitamin B_1 (thiamin), over 5% of the RDV for vitamin B_3 (niacin), 5% of the RDV of phosphorus, and over 4% of the RDV for both magnesium and folate.

Carrots contain carotenoids, natural fat-soluble pigments found in certain plants that provide their bright coloration and serve as antioxidants and a source for vitamin A activity. These carotenoids are associated with protection from heart disease and cancer, improved night vision, and improved blood sugar regulation. Research also suggests that vitamin A may reduce the risk of emphysema, even among smokers or those who are exposed to secondhand smoke.

Another phytonutrient found in carrots, called falcarinol, may also play a role in protection against colon cancer, according to the results of a study published in the February 2005 issue of the *Journal of Agriculture and Food Chemistry*.

Peppers

Bell peppers come in a dazzling palette of reds, yellows, oranges, greens, purples, and nearly blacks. Bell peppers have a sweet, rather than hot, taste. The compound capsaicin, which is responsible for the heat of chili and jalapeño peppers, is missing in these milder varieties.

Peppers are loaded with potent antioxidant vitamins A and C. For example, one cup of raw red peppers contains 291% RDV of vitamin C and 104% RDV of vitamin A. Peppers are also high in vitamin K (nearly 20% RDV) and B_6 (over 11% RDV). They are also excellent sources of fiber (nearly 2 grams per cup). Peppers also have significant amounts of molybdenum (a trace mineral that plays a role in three enzyme systems involved in the metabolism of carbohydrates, fats, and proteins, and is also found in tooth enamel), manganese, folate, potassium, vitamin B_1 (thiamin), vitamin E, tryptophan, and copper.

Like carrots and oranges, red, yellow, and orange peppers contain carotenoids, natural fat-soluble pigments found in certain plants that provide their bright coloration and serve as antioxidants and a source for vitamin A activity. These carotenoids are associated with protection from heart disease and cancer, improved night vision, and improved blood sugar regulation. Research also suggests that vitamin A may reduce the risk of emphysema, even among smokers or those who are exposed to secondhand smoke.

The vitamin B_6 and folic acid in peppers play an important part in reducing levels of homocysteine and protecting the cardiovascular system. The fiber in peppers can help lower cholesterol levels and may help to prevent colorectal cancer. Yellow peppers are rich in lutein and zeaxanthin, phytonutrients that help protect against macular degeneration, a cause of blindness.

Shiitake Mushrooms

Used medicinally by the Chinese for thousands of years, shiitake mushrooms have a rich flavor that has made them a favorite ingredient of American cooks. Despite their exotic name and appearance, they are easily found in most supermarkets.

Shiitake mushrooms are a good source of iron. Eight ounces of raw mushrooms contain nearly 20% of the RDV of iron. They are also good sources of vitamin C (10% RDV), protein (10% RDV), and fiber (about 2½ grams).

Lentinan, a polysaccharide found in shiitake mushrooms, has been studied in Japan as a treatment for cancer, and studies suggest that it may activate the immune system's tumor-fighting T cells. Another Japanese study demonstrates the effective cholesterol-reducing properties of eritadenine, an active component of shiitake mushrooms.

Shiitake mushrooms also contain the highest amounts of a powerful antioxidant called ergothioneine. Even better, this potent antioxidant is not destroyed when the mushrooms are cooked.

Fresh shiitake mushrooms will keep about one week when loosely stored in a paper bag and refrigerated. Dried mushrooms should be stored in a tightly sealed container and may be refrigerated or frozen for up to six months.

Tomatoes

Fresh, ripe tomatoes are one of the tastiest treats of the summer. But the benefits of this Power Food can be enjoyed all year by using tomato pastes, sauces, and even sun-dried tomatoes. The bright red, yellow, even orange colors of fresh tomatoes indicate the presence of carotenes, antioxidants with a host of health benefits. It is important to choose organic tomatoes, as the powerful carotenoid antioxidant lycopene can be up to three times higher in organic tomatoes than in conventionally grown tomatoes.

Tomatoes are loaded with healthy vitamins and trace minerals. One cup of ripe, raw tomato provides loads of vitamin C (57% RDV), vitamin A (22% RDV), vitamin K (13% RDV), and molybdenum (a trace mineral that plays a role in three enzyme systems involved in the metabolism of carbohydrates, fats, and proteins, and is also found in tooth enamel; 12% RDV). Tomatoes also contain ample amounts of B vitamins: B_1, B_2, B_3, B_5, and B_6, as well as potassium, manganese, fiber, chromium, folate, magnesium, iron, vitamin E, tryptophan, and even a small amount of protein.

The antioxidant lycopene has been the subject of much interest over the past several years. Studies have linked its antioxidant properties to the protection of DNA, the prevention of heart disease, and protection against cancers, including colorectal, breast, endometrial, lung, and pancreatic cancer.

Tomatoes are also loaded with carotenoids, natural fat-soluble pigments found in certain plants that provide their bright coloration and serve as antioxidants and a source for vitamin A activity. These carotenoids are associated with protection from heart disease and cancer, improved night vision, and improved blood sugar regulation. Research also suggests that vitamin A may reduce the risk of emphysema, even among smokers or those who are exposed to secondhand smoke.

The vitamin K found in tomatoes is an important part of maintaining bone health, and studies suggest that the riboflavin (vitamin B_2) in tomatoes may be helpful in reducing the frequency of migraine attacks.

When cooking or juicing tomatoes, be sure to use the whole tomato, including the peel, to gain the most benefits from the synergy of all the nutrients that are present. Whenever possible, make your own tomato sauces and pastes.

Leafy Greens

The rich green color of leafy greens is the indicator of the antioxidants that make these vegetables one of the best Power Foods to incorporate into your daily diet. Calorie for calorie, some of these greens are the most nutrient-packed foods you can eat. The selection of greens is wide; there's no reason to become bored with a simple salad day after day. In the recipes that follow, I've introduced spinach, kale, arugula, Swiss chard, cabbage, collard greens, and watercress as power-packed ingredients in everything from juices to soups, from appetizers to entrées.

Kale may be one of the healthiest greens for your bones. Just one cup of cooked kale contains over 1,300% (that's right, over 1,300%)

of the RDV of vitamin K. Kale also is high in calcium (25% RDV) and is a good source of manganese (84% RDV), which helps promote bone density. Kale is the top leafy green source of carotenoids, natural fat-soluble pigments found in certain plants that provide their bright coloration and serve as antioxidants and a source for vitamin A activity. These carotenoids are associated with protection from heart disease and cancer, improved night vision, and improved blood sugar regulation. Research also suggests that vitamin A may reduce the risk of emphysema, even among smokers or those who are exposed to secondhand smoke.

One cup of Swiss chard supplies nearly 35% of the RDV of potassium and may help lower blood pressure. Swiss chard is the number-one leafy green source of iron (22% RDV) and an excellent source of vitamin C (52% RDV).

One cup of cooked spinach offers 35% of the RDV of iron, to boost energy and improve circulatory health, and over 1,100% of the RDV of vitamin K for bone health.

All leafy greens contain lutein and zeaxanthin, phytonutrients that help protect against macular degeneration, a cause of blindness.

Soy

A staple of Asian cooking, soy has gained popularity among cooks for its versatility. Although it's a legume, I have listed soy as a separate Power Food because of its extensive and well-researched health benefits and because it is used in such a wide range of forms, from cooked beans and sprouts, to tofu and tempeh, to nondairy products like milks, cottage cheese, cheese, yogurt, and ice creams. No other legume can be used in so many delicious ways.

A one-cup serving of cooked soybeans has 300 calories and packs a whopping 29 grams of protein. Soy also offers high concentrations of molybdenum (a trace mineral that plays a role in three enzyme systems involved in the metabolism of carbohydrates, fats, and proteins, and is also found in tooth enamel; 172% RDV). Soy also contains tryptophan (115% RDV), an amino acid that occurs in proteins and is essential for growth and normal metabolism. Tryptophan is a precursor of niacin, which helps the body produce serotonin, a chemical that acts as a calming agent in the brain and plays a role in sleep regulation.

Soy is an excellent replacement for animal protein, containing high values of iron (49% RDV), and essential omega-3 fatty acids (41% RDV). Other beneficial components of soy include phosphorus (42% RDV), fiber (41% RDV), and significant amounts of magnesium, copper, vitamin B_2 (riboflavin), and potassium.

Studies show that consumption of soy may play a role in a wide range of health benefits, from helping to lower blood cholesterol and promote good (HDL) cholesterol, to increasing cardiac function, strengthening bone mass, stabilizing blood sugar, and protecting against diabetes-related kidney and heart disease. The fiber in soy has been credited with helping to prevent colon, breast, and prostate cancer, and helping to relieve symptoms of irritable bowel syndrome.

Soy can be used in nearly any recipe and can take on the flavors and textures of any style of cooking. Whether you are using soymilk in a breakfast smoothie, snacking on lightly boiled edamame, grilling tofu, or whipping up a batch of chili con tempeh, when you create dishes with soy you are creating real health benefits.

Whole Grains

Delicious and energy-rich grains are an important part of a healthy eating plan. By now most Americans know that whole-grain breads and pastas are healthier than those made with refined white flour, and that brown rice offers greater health benefits than white rice. But there are many more grains other than wheat that we should incorporate into a healthy diet. Rather than single out one grain as having more benefits than another, I choose to consider all whole grains Power Foods. Packed with fiber and rich in heart-healthy nutrients, whole grains can be enjoyed in many forms. In the recipes that follow, I introduce some grains that you may not be familiar with, which can be used to create tasty, hearty, and satisfying recipes.

I provide delicious ways for using spelt, a grain that provides 75% of your RDV for vitamin B_2 (riboflavin), which reduces the frequency of migraines and helps process calories from carbohydrates, protein, and fat. Your body needs it for growth and red cell production, and adequate riboflavin intake promotes healthy skin and good vision.

Barley is an excellent source of selenium (54% RDV), which studies suggest may reduce the risk of colon cancer, and tryptophan (38%

RDV), a precursor of niacin, which helps the body produce serotonin, a chemical that acts as a calming agent in the brain and plays a role in sleep regulation.

Millet is a seedlike grain that provides manganese (33% RDV), magnesium (26% RDV), and phosphorus (24% RDV). Magnesium has been shown to lower blood pressure and reduce the risk of heart attack. Phosphorus is an important component of nucleic acid, a building block of DNA.

Two other foods that are often considered grains and are used as such in recipes (though they technically are not) are buckwheat (a fruit seed) and quinoa (a relative of leafy green vegetables).

All whole grains are rich in fiber, an important dietary component. Consumption of fiber plays a role in the prevention of gallstones, increased cardiac health, the regulation of blood sugar, lowered cholesterol (and increased good, HDL cholesterol) levels and protection from cancers, especially colorectal cancer.

When cooking, use whole grain flours. Look for whole grain pastas and experiment with a variety of grains to find the tastes you most enjoy.

SECTION 2

RECIPES

Chapter   Three

BEVERAGES

NOTE: When juicing fruits and vegetables, even when using organic produce, wash thoroughly with a produce wash. Unless otherwise noted, fruits and vegetables should be juiced with their rinds, peels, and skins, which contain high concentrations of important vitamins and fiber. There are important exceptions to this rule of thumb, however. Whether organic or conventionally grown, unless otherwise noted, bananas, melons, onions, garlic, ginger, pineapples, mangoes, and guavas should all be peeled before juicing. If you are not using organic produce, remove rinds and peel skins from citrus fruits and vegetables.

When adding supplements to juices and smoothies, break open capsules and use powders when possible; supplements in tablet form may be added directly to juice mixtures, or blended with smoothies. Be sure to stir in supplements thoroughly, and beware: some supplements can have a strong sulfurlike taste.

Juices can be diluted with water and smoothies may be diluted with soy or rice milk, or sweetened with coconut milk to suit individual tastes.

Several recipes call for Gary Null's Red Stuff or Gary Null's Green Stuff. These supplements are available online at www.garynull.com.

8 SPROUT JUICE

POWER 2

1 cup alfalfa sprouts
1 cup buckwheat sprouts
1 cup clover sprouts
1 cup crunchy sprouts
1 cup lentil sprouts
1 cup mustard sprouts
1 cup radish sprouts
1 cup sunflower sprouts
4–5 medium radishes
1 bunch kale, chopped
2 apples, cored and quartered
1 cucumber, quartered
1 teaspoon sprout powder or blend of sprout powder
2 ounces wheatgrass juice*

1. Push alfalfa, buckwheat, clover, crunchy, lentil, mustard, radish, and sunflower sprouts, then radishes, kale, apples, and cucumber through the juicer.
2. Add sprout powder and wheatgrass juice to the juice mixture, and stir well.
3. Dilute mixture with spring water to taste.
4. Serve immediately.

MAKES 5 SERVINGS.

*Chef's Note: Wheatgrass can be juiced by using a special wheatgrass press. You can also make wheatgrass juice by squeezing the grass into clusters with your hands and juicing these clusters through a traditional fruit and vegetable juicer. If your juicer can't process wheatgrass, you can buy wheatgrass in powder form. One teaspoon of the powder is equal to 2 ounces of fresh wheatgrass.

A TASTE OF EDEN

POWER 2

2 mangoes, peeled, pitted, and quartered
1 papaya, peeled, pitted, and quartered
1 tangerine, quartered
¼ pineapple, rind removed, cored and quartered
1 cup cherries, pitted
1 cup rice milk
2 tablespoons soy protein powder
1 large lime, sliced into ¼-inch-thick half-moons, as garnish (optional)

1. Push mangoes, papaya, tangerine, pineapple, and cherries through the juicer.
2. In a blender, combine the rice milk, protein powder, and the juice mixture, and blend until smooth.
3. Pour into a glass and garnish with lime, if desired.
4. Serve immediately.

MAKES 1 SERVING.

ALMOND SHAKE

POWER 2

1 cup soymilk or rice milk
6 dates, pitted
½ cup raw almonds, whole
1 cup cherries, pitted

1. In a blender, combine soymilk or rice milk with the dates, almonds, and cherries, and blend until smooth.
2. Serve chilled.

MAKES 1 SERVING.

ANTIAGING ELIXIR

POWER 3

1 cup blueberries
1 cup purple grapes, with seeds
1 cup watermelon, rind removed, cubed
2 medium zucchini, sliced
1 medium tomato, quartered
1 cup spring water
2 tablespoons soy protein powder
500 mg L-carnosine
100 mg ginkgo biloba
100 mg glutathione
100 mg phosphatidylserine

1. Push blueberries, grapes, watermelon, zucchini, and tomato through the juicer.
2. Add the spring water, protein powder, and supplements to the juice mixture, and stir well.
3. Serve immediately.

MAKES 1–2 SERVINGS.

AVOCADO, ALMOND, CHERRY SHAKE

POWER 2

1 avocado, peeled and diced
1 cup cherries, pitted, fresh or frozen
3 tablespoons raw almonds, whole
½ cup plain soymilk (or rice milk)

1. In a blender, combine avocado, cherries, and almonds, and blend until smooth.
2. Add soymilk (or rice milk) to mixture, and blend well.
3. Serve immediately.

MAKES 1 SERVING.

BANANA DATE CREAM SHAKE

POWER 2

2 cups cantaloupe, peeled and cubed
2 bananas, peeled
½ cup dried dates
¼ cup agar-agar
½ cup French vanilla soy creamer

1. Push the cantaloupe through the juicer.
2. In a blender, combine the bananas, dates, agar-agar, and soy creamer.
3. Add the cantaloupe juice to the blender mixture, and blend until smooth.
4. Serve immediately.

MAKES 2 SERVINGS.

BANANA SPLIT SHAKE

POWER 1

1 banana, peeled
1/4 cup strawberries, hulled
1/4 cup walnuts, whole
1/2 cup rice milk
1 scoop carob Rice Dream powder

1. In a blender, combine banana, strawberries, walnuts, and rice milk. Blend until smooth.
2. Add Rice Dream powder and blend well.
3. Serve immediately.

MAKES 1 SERVING.

BERRY CITRUS SLUSH

POWER 2

8 oranges, quartered
2 limes, quartered
2 cups mixed berries (strawberries, raspberries, blackberries, pitted
cherries, and blueberries)
1 grapefruit, quartered
1 cup spring water
1 large lime, sliced into ¼-inch-thick half-moons, as garnish (optional)

1. Push the oranges, limes, berries, and grapefruit through the juicer.
2. Combine 1¼ cups of juice with 1 cup spring water and set aside in the refrigerator.
3. Pour the remaining juice into 4 ice cube trays and freeze for 1–2 hours, or until frozen.
4. Transfer the frozen cubes to a blender or food processor, and blend with the refrigerated juice until slushy in consistency.
5. Pour into tall glasses with straws and garnish with lime slices, if desired.
6. Serve immediately.

MAKES 3 SERVINGS.

BLOOD BUILDER

POWER 2

½ cup carrots
½ lemon, halved
1 small piece organic burdock root
2 apples, cored and quartered
1 pear, cored and quartered
2 cups spinach, chopped
1 cup collard greens, chopped
1 cup watercress, chopped
1 cup kale, chopped
¾ cup dandelion roots, chopped
1 cup spring water
4 ounces aloe vera concentrate
1 tablespoon blackstrap molasses
1,000 mg vitamin C
10 drops yellowdock
800 mcg folic acid
300 mcg biotin
1,000 mcg vitamin B$_{12}$
50 mg B-complex vitamin
coenzyme Q10, as directed by manufacturer

1. Push the carrots, lemon, burdock root, apples, pear, spinach, collard greens, watercress, kale, and dandelion roots through the juicer.
2. Add the spring water, aloe vera concentrate, molasses, and supplements to the juice mixture, and stir well.
3. Serve immediately.

MAKES 3 SERVINGS.

BOO TO THE FLU

POWER 3

1 cup apricots, pitted
8 ounces soy yogurt
2 bananas, peeled and frozen
1 cup raspberries
2 cups strawberries, hulled
1 cup rice milk
1/2 teaspoon Probiotic Powder
3 tablespoons agave or other sweetener
1 teaspoon coconut oil
1 teaspoon glutamine
1 tablespoon flax oil
10,000 IU vitamin A
1,000 mg vitamin C
500 mg quercetin
500 mg NAC (N-acetylcysteine)
200 mg olive leaf extract
100 mg echinacea
100 mg astragalus
cat's claw, as directed by manufacturer
1/2 teaspoon slippery elm (optional)

1. In a blender or food processor, combine apricots, soy yogurt, bananas, raspberries, and strawberries, and blend until smooth.
2. Add rice milk, Probiotic Powder, sweetener, coconut oil, and supplements, and blend until smooth.
3. Serve immediately.

MAKES 2 SERVINGS.

BRAIN REJUVENATOR

POWER 2

1 cup blueberries
2 tangerines, quartered
2 mangoes, peeled, diced, and pitted
1 cup rice milk
12 walnuts, chopped
100 mg ginseng (dried herb or contents of capsule)
100 mg ginkgo biloba (dried herb or contents of capsule)
1 tablespoon flaxseed oil
1 tablespoon coconut oil
200 mg phosphatidylserine
500 mg L-carnosine
300 mg coenzyme Q10
500 mg R-alpha-lipoic acid
300 mg acetyl-L-carnitine
dash turmeric
dash cayenne

1. Push blueberries, tangerines, and mangoes through the juicer.
2. Pour juice into a blender.
3. Add rice milk, walnuts, ginseng, ginkgo, and all other supplements, and blend to a smooth consistency.
4. Serve immediately.

MAKES 1 SERVING.

BRIGHT EYES

POWER 2

1 cup collard greens, chopped
1 cup spinach, chopped
2 pints blueberries
4 cucumbers, peeled and quartered
160 mg bilberry extract
1 tablespoon flaxseed oil
1 cup coconut milk
1/2 teaspoon turmeric
10,000 IU vitamin A
50 mg B-complex vitamin
200 mg coenzyme Q10
1,000 mg vitamin C
100 mg grape seed extract
200 mg alpha-lipoic acid
500 mg NAC (N-acetylcysteine)
500 mg glutathione
100 mg ginkgo biloba
20 mg astaxanthin
20 mg lutein
20 mg lycopene
20 mg zeaxanthin

1. In a blender, combine collard greens, spinach, blueberries, and cucumbers, and blend until smooth.
2. Add bilberry extract, flaxseed oil, coconut milk, turmeric, and supplements, and blend until creamy.
3. Serve immediately.

MAKES 2 SERVINGS.

CANTALOUPE AND SWEET POTATO JUICE

¹/₂ cantaloupe, rind removed, cubed
2 sweet potatoes, quartered
1 pear, quartered

1. Push cantaloupe, sweet potatoes, and pear through the juicer, and stir juice well.
2. Serve immediately.

MAKES 1 SERVING.

CELERY SIP

POWER 2

6 stalks celery
1 parsnip, top removed, sliced
1 apple, sliced
1 large tomato
ground ginger, to taste

1. Push the celery, parsnip, apple, and tomato through the juicer.
2. Add a dash of ginger to taste, and stir well.
3. Serve immediately.

MAKES 1 SERVING.

CHERRY JAMMIN' JUICE

POWER 2

3 cups orange juice
1 cup frozen cherries, pitted
1/2 cup ice cubes
2 tablespoons cranberry juice concentrate
1 tablespoon soy protein powder
1/4 teaspoon cinnamon

1. In a blender, combine orange juice, frozen cherries, ice cubes, cranberry juice concentrate, protein powder, and cinnamon, and blend until smooth.
2. Serve immediately.

MAKES 2 SERVINGS.

CHERRY PEAR CHILL

POWER 1

2 cups pears, quartered
4 cups pineapple, rind removed, cored, and cut into 1-inch cubes
4 cups frozen cherries, pitted
4 bananas, peeled and frozen
2 cups coconut milk
1 tablespoon flaxseed oil (optional)
10 ice cubes

1. Push the pears and pineapple through the juicer.
2. In a blender, combine the juice mixture with the cherries, bananas, coconut milk, flaxseed oil, and ice, and blend until smooth.
3. Serve immediately.

MAKES 8 SERVINGS.

CHI JUICE*

P O W E R   2

½ large daikon radish, peeled and sliced
1 cup Chinese go chi berries, goji, or wolfberries
2-inch piece gingerroot, peeled
2 ounces Chinese lotus root
½ bok choy
1 cup Japanese mitsuba, with stems and leaves
2 apples, cored and quartered
1 cup green or white tea, chilled
1 capsule each fo-ti teng, gotu kola, ginseng
pinch sea vegetable

1. Push daikon, go chi berries, gingerroot, lotus root, bok choy, mitsuba, and apples through the juicer.
2. Add green or white tea, the contents of each capsule, and sea vegetable to the juice mixture, and stir well.
3. Serve immediately.

MAKES 3 SERVINGS.

*Chef's Note: You'll need to find an Asian market or a specialty grocer for these ingredients.

CHILL OUT

POWER 1

1 cucumber, quartered
3 stalks celery
1 apple, cored and quartered
1 cup spring water
500 mg calcium
500 mg magnesium
200 mg threonine
200 mg St. John's wort capsule
50 mg valerian capsule
25 mg chamomile capsule
¼ teaspoon nutmeg
¼ teaspoon cinnamon
1-inch piece gingerroot, peeled

1. Push the cucumber, celery, and apple through the juicer.
2. Combine the juice mixture and spring water in a blender.
3. Open supplement capsules and add powder, nutmeg, cinnamon, and gingerroot to juice mixture, and blend well.
4. Serve immediately.

MAKES 3 SERVINGS.

CHLOROPHYLL FOR LIFE

POWER 1

2 cups sunflower sprouts
2 cups collard greens, chopped
2 cups kale, chopped, without stems
2 cups broccoli crowns
1 apple, cored and quartered (optional)
1 cup white tea, chilled
2 ounces wheatgrass juice*
2 tablespoons Gary Null's Green Stuff
1 tablespoon Gary Null's Greens & Grains

1. Push the sprouts, collard greens, kale, broccoli, and apple through the juicer.
2. Add the white tea, wheatgrass juice, and powders to the juice mixture, and stir well.
3. Serve immediately.

MAKES 4 SERVINGS.

*Chef's Note: If your juicer can't process wheatgrass, you can buy wheatgrass powder. One teaspoon of the powder is equal to 2 ounces of fresh wheatgrass.

CHOLESTEROL BUSTER

POWER 2

10 stalks celery
1 grapefruit, peeled and quartered
3 apples, cored and quartered
2 cloves garlic, peeled
1 cup red cabbage, chopped
1 teaspoon flaxseed oil
1 teaspoon pomegranate concentrate
1 teaspoon oat bran or Gary Null's Friendly Fiber
1 tablespoon liquid lecithin
pinch cayenne
1,000 mg vitamin C
500 mg calcium
500 mg magnesium
500 mg L-carnitine
200 mg coenzyme Q10
400 IU vitamin E
50 mg B-complex vitamin
10 mg polycosanol
proteolytic enzymes, as directed by manufacturer

1. Push the celery, grapefruit, apples, garlic, and cabbage through the juicer.
2. Add the flaxseed oil, pomegranate concentrate, oat bran, lecithin, cayenne, and supplements, and mix until smooth.
3. Serve immediately.

MAKES 2 SERVINGS.

COLON CLEANSE

P O W E R   3

¹/₈ cup ginger, peeled
¹/₄ watermelon, rind removed, cubed
2 cups sunflower sprouts
¹/₂ pint blueberries
1 lime, peeled and quartered
1 lemon, peeled and quartered
¹/₄ cup radishes
2 cloves garlic, peeled
1 cup fresh cherries, pitted
¹/₄ cup aloe vera juice or concentrate
1 tablespoon Gary Null's Friendly Fiber
1 teaspoon flaxseed oil
1 teaspoon blackberry concentrate
¹/₄ teaspoon vitamin C (approximately 1,000 mg)

1. Push the ginger, watermelon, sprouts, blueberries, lime, lemon, radishes, and garlic through the juicer.
2. In a blender, combine cherries, aloe vera, Friendly Fiber, flaxseed oil, blackberry concentrate, and vitamin C, and blend until smooth.
3. Add the juice mixture to the blender mixture, and blend well.
4. Serve immediately.

MAKES 3 SERVINGS.

COOL KIWI COOLER

2 cups purified water
4 green tea bags
¼ cup agave or other sweetener (optional)
1 pineapple, rind removed, cored and cubed
4 kiwis, peeled and quartered
1 lime, peeled and quartered
1 grapefruit, peeled and quartered
10 ice cubes
4 large kiwis, sliced into ½-inch-thick cross-sections, as garnish
   (optional)
fresh mint, to taste (optional)

1. In a small saucepan, combine the water and tea bags over moderate heat and simmer, covered, for 8–10 minutes, or until fully brewed. Stir in the agave, if desired, until well combined, and set aside to cool completely.
2. Push the pineapple, kiwis, lime, and grapefruit through the juicer.
3. In a large pitcher, combine the juice mixture, tea, and ice. Stir together until well combined.
4. Pour into glasses and garnish with kiwi slices and mint, if desired.
5. Serve immediately.

MAKES 8 SERVINGS.

CRANBERRY CITRUS SPRITZER

POWER 1

4 large tangerines, quartered
2 limes, quartered
1 lemon, quartered
1 cup unsweetened cranberry juice
1 cup blueberries
1 tablespoon cherry concentrate
1 tablespoon pomegranate concentrate
1/4 cup agave or other sweetener
1 teaspoon cinnamon
4 cups purified water
20 ice cubes
1 quart carbonated spring water
1 large kiwi, sliced into 1/4-inch half-moons, as garnish (optional)

1. Push the tangerines, limes, and lemon through the juicer.
2. In a blender, combine the juice mixture, cranberry juice, blueberries, cherry and pomegranate concentrates, agave, cinnamon, water, and half the ice cubes. Blend until well combined.
3. Add carbonated water and stir.
4. Pour into glasses filled with the remaining ice cubes and garnish with kiwi slices, if desired.
5. Serve immediately.

MAKES 8 SERVINGS.

CRUCIFEROUS MEDLEY

POWER 1

1 broccoli crown, chopped
½ pint Brussels sprouts
4 cucumbers, sliced lengthwise
2 cups red cabbage, chopped
2 cups cauliflower
3 apples, cored and quartered
2 cups asparagus, chopped
1 cup mustard sprouts
½ cup radishes
1 teaspoon flaxseed oil

1. Push broccoli, Brussels sprouts, cucumbers, cabbage, cauliflower, apples, asparagus, sprouts, and radishes through the juicer.
2. In a blender, combine juice mixture and flaxseed oil, and blend until smooth.
3. Serve immediately.

MAKES 3 SERVINGS.

DEEP PURPLE

P O W E R   2

1 cup red grapes, with seeds
2 medium black plums, pitted
¼ head red cabbage, chopped
1 cup blueberries
1 cup blackberries
1 cup spring water
1 serving (1 teaspoon) Gary Null's Red Stuff

1. Push the grapes, plums, cabbage, blueberries, and blackberries through the juicer.
2. Add spring water and Red Stuff, and stir well.
3. Serve immediately.

MAKES 2 SERVINGS.

ENZYME FOR LIFE

POWER 2

1 cup wild blackberries
1 papaya, peeled, pitted, and cubed
¼ pineapple, rind removed, cubed
1 cup strawberries, hulled and halved
¼ head cabbage, chopped
½ kiwi, peeled and quartered
1 cup spring water
1 teaspoon cranberry concentrate
1 teaspoon dark cherry concentrate
1 teaspoon pomegranate concentrate
1 teaspoon grape concentrate
dash nutmeg
1 teaspoon nondairy acidophilus
1 tablespoon Gary Null's Red Stuff

1. Push the blackberries, papaya, pineapple, strawberries, cabbage, and kiwi through the juicer.
2. Pour the spring water and juice mixture into a blender and add cranberry, cherry, pomegranate, and grape concentrates, nutmeg, and supplements, and blend well.
3. Serve immediately.

MAKES 2 SERVINGS.

EXOTIC HEALTH SHAKE

POWER 3

2 cups coconut milk
1 cup soy ice cream
1/2 cup blueberries
1/2 cup cherries, pitted
1/2 cup banana, peeled and sliced
1 cup raw macadamia nuts, whole
2 tablespoons soy protein powder
6 ounces rice milk or soymilk
1 teaspoon flaxseed oil

1. In a blender, combine coconut milk, soy ice cream, blueberries, cherries, banana, macadamia nuts, protein powder, rice milk or soymilk, and flaxseed oil, and blend until smooth.
2. Serve immediately.

MAKES 2 SERVINGS.

EXTREME BERRY SHAKE

POWER 3

2 cups rice milk or soymilk
1 cup fresh or frozen cherries, pitted, or blueberries, raspberries,
*   strawberries, or blackberries*
1 banana, peeled
3 tablespoons pure maple syrup
1 cup ice cubes
1 tablespoon soy protein powder

1. In a blender, combine rice milk or soymilk, berries, banana, maple syrup, ice cubes, and protein powder, and blend until smooth.
2. Serve immediately.

MAKES 2 SERVINGS.

FATIGUE FIGHTER

2 parsnips, tops removed, sliced
2 cucumbers, peeled, seeded, and sliced
1 pear, cored and quartered
1 cup green tea, chilled
¼ teaspoon bee propolis
1 teaspoon chia seeds
1,000 mg glutamine
500 mg carnitine
200 mg coenzyme Q10
100 mg ginseng

1. Push the parsnips, cucumbers, and pear through the juicer.
2. Add the green tea, bee propolis, chia seeds, and supplements to the juice mixture, and stir well.
3. Serve immediately.

MAKES 1 SERVING.

FOR KIDS ONLY

P O W E R   3

1 orange, peeled
2 kiwis, quartered
1 cup strawberries, hulled and stemmed
2 passion fruits, quartered
2 tangerines, peeled and quartered
2 cups spring water
1 banana, peeled
1 teaspoon cherry concentrate
1 teaspoon wild blueberry concentrate
12 ice cubes

1. Push the orange, kiwis, strawberries, passion fruits, and tangerines through the juicer.
2. In a blender, combine juice with spring water, banana, and cherry and wild blueberry concentrates, and blend well.
3. Pour into tall glasses filled with ice.
4. Serve immediately.

MAKES 3 SERVINGS.

FRUITY SPRITZER

POWER 1

1 mango, peeled, pitted, and cubed
4 cups watermelon, rind removed, cubed
½ pineapple, rind removed, cored, and cubed
1 cup raspberries
¼-inch piece gingerroot, peeled
½ cup seltzer
1 cup ice

1. Push the mango, watermelon, pineapple, raspberries, and ginger through the juicer.
2. Pour juice mixture into blender and add seltzer and ice, and blend well.
3. Serve chilled.

MAKES 2 SERVINGS.

GALLBLADDER FLUSH

POWER 1

1 cup alfalfa sprouts
3 cups cabbage, any color, chopped
2 apples, cored and quartered
1 cup kale, chopped
1 cup spinach, chopped
1 lemon, quartered
1 cup green tea, chilled
4 ounces aloe vera concentrate
3 drops wild oregano oil
3 tablespoons olive oil
1 tablespoon flaxseed oil
1 peppermint oil capsule
½ tablespoon turmeric
1 tablespoon lecithin granules
L-Glycine, as directed by manufacturer
1,000 mg vitamin C
100 mg taurine
50 mg B-complex vitamin

1. Push the sprouts, cabbage, apples, kale, spinach, and lemon through the juicer.
2. In a blender, combine the juice mixture with the green tea, aloe vera concentrate, oregano oil, olive oil, flaxseed oil, and all supplements, and blend well.
3. Serve immediately.

MAKES 2 SERVINGS.

GRAPES AND CONCENTRATES

POWER 2

4 cups red grapes, with seeds
2 cups watercress, chopped
2 cups kale, chopped
2 cups spring water
1 tablespoon pomegranate concentrate
1 tablespoon wild blueberry concentrate

1. Push the red grapes, watercress, and kale through the juicer.
2. Add the water and pomegranate and blueberry concentrates to the juice mixture, and stir well.
3. Serve immediately.

MAKES 2 SERVINGS.

GREEN MONSTER

POWER 1

2 cups Swiss chard, chopped
2 cups kale, chopped
2 cups parsley, chopped
1 cup spinach, chopped
1 apple, cored and quartered
1 cup broccoli, chopped
¹/₂ head cauliflower, chopped
4 stalks celery
1 cup asparagus, chopped
1 cup spring water
1 tablespoon Gary Null's Green Stuff

1. Push the Swiss chard, kale, parsley, spinach, apple, broccoli, cauliflower, celery, and asparagus through the juicer.
2. Blend spring water and Green Stuff into the juice mixture, and stir well.
3. Serve immediately.

MAKES 2 SERVINGS.

GUM PLEASER

POWER 1

1 cup spinach, chopped
¹/₂ cup parsley, chopped
1 pineapple, rind removed, cubed
2 stalks celery
1 apple, cored and quartered
1 parsnip, top removed, chopped
1 cup spring water
3 drops wild oregano oil
300 mg coenzyme Q10 capsule
1,000 mg vitamin C
500 mg quercetin
1 tablespoon raw chocolate or cocoa (pure)
dash cayenne

1. Push spinach, parsley, pineapple, celery, apple, and parsnip through the juicer.
2. Add the spring water, oregano oil, supplements, chocolate, and cayenne to the juice mixture, and stir well.
3. Serve immediately.

MAKES 2 SERVINGS.

HAWAIIAN JUICE

POWER 1

1 pint blueberries
1 pint strawberries, hulled and halved
1 cup pineapple, rind removed, cubed
1 papaya, peeled and cubed
1 cup mango, peeled, pitted, and halved
1 cup raspberries
1 cup goji berries
2 cups spring water
ice cubes

1. Push blueberries, strawberries, pineapple, papaya, mango, raspberries, and goji berries through the juicer.
2. Combine juice with spring water and stir well.
3. Pour into tall glasses over ice.
4. Serve immediately.

MAKES 2 SERVINGS.

HEALTHY EYES

POWER 2

1 cup red or purple grapes, with seeds
1 apricot, pitted and halved
½ pint huckleberries or mixed berries
1 yam, quartered
1 cup spinach, chopped
1 pint blueberries
3 cups cantaloupe, rind removed, cubed
1 cup spring water
500 mg quercetin
100 mg bilberry
20 mg lutein
10 mg lycopene
5 mg zeaxanthin

1. Push grapes, apricot, huckleberries or mixed berries, yam, spinach, blueberries, and cantaloupe through the juicer.
2. In a blender, combine the juice with the spring water and supplements, and blend well.
3. Serve immediately.

MAKES 2 SERVINGS.

HEALTHY LUNGS

POWER 2

3 cloves garlic, peeled
2 large carrots, tops removed, sliced lengthwise
1 apple, cored and quartered
1 avocado, peeled, quartered, and pitted
1/2 guava fruit, peeled, seeded, and quartered
2 cups white tea, chilled
2 teaspoons Gary Null's Green Stuff
2 teaspoons Gary Null's Red Stuff
1,000 mg NAC (N-acetylcysteine)
1,000 mg vitamin C
500 mg magnesium
500 mg calcium
500 mg quercetin
200 mg alfa-lipoic acid
300 mg coenzyme Q10
500 mg GLA (gamma-linolenic acid)
30 mg green tea
15 mg zinc

1. Push the garlic, carrots, apple, avocado, and guava through the juicer.
2. In a blender, combine the white tea and supplements with the juice mixture, and blend well.
3. Serve immediately.

MAKES 2 SERVINGS.

HEALTHY MILKSHAKE

POWER 1

3 cups soymilk
¹/₄ cup grapefruit juice
¹/₄ cup raisins
¹/₄ cup pine nuts
1 scoop soy protein powder
1 tablespoon pure maple syrup
1 teaspoon coconut flakes

1. In a blender, combine soymilk, grapefruit juice, raisins, pine nuts, protein powder, maple syrup, and coconut, and blend until mixed completely.
2. Serve immediately.

MAKES 3 SERVINGS.

HEALTHY PROSTATE

POWER 2

1 cup asparagus, chopped
1 cup cauliflower, cubed
1 cup apricot, pitted, halved
1 cup fresh rosemary
1 cup spinach, chopped
1 cup broccoli sprouts
1 cup sunflower sprouts
1/2 apple
1/2 cup parsley, chopped
1/2 cup cranberries
2 tablespoons pumpkin seeds
2 cups green tea, chilled
1 tablespoon Gary Null's Green
    Stuff

1 teaspoon flaxseed oil
1/8 teaspoon turmeric
pinch ginger
400 IU vitamin D
200 mg green tea concentrate
150 mg saw palmetto
100 mg cernitin
100 mg stinging nettles
50 mg pygeum africanum
10 mg lycopene
10 mg uva ursi
2 mg boron

1. Push the asparagus, cauliflower, apricot, rosemary, spinach, broccoli sprouts, sunflower sprouts, apple, parsley, and cranberries through the juicer.
2. Using a food processor, grind the pumpkin seeds into a very fine powder.
3. Add the pumpkin seed powder, green tea, and supplements to the juice mixture, and stir well.
4. Serve immediately.

MAKES 2 SERVINGS.

HOT POTATO COOL TOMATO

POWER 1

3 medium tomatoes, quartered
3 potatoes, quartered
2 apples, cored and quartered
3 red plums, pitted
1/8 teaspoon cayenne

1. Push the tomatoes, potatoes, apples, and plums through the juicer.
2. Add cayenne pepper to the juice mixture and stir well.
3. Serve immediately.

MAKES 1 SERVING.

I HAVE A HANGOVER CURE

1 lemon, quartered
1 lime, quartered
1 grapefruit, quartered
1 cucumber, sliced lengthwise
4 stalks celery
2 cups white tea, chilled
4 ounces aloe vera juice
1/2 teaspoon cayenne
1 teaspoon Gary Null's Green Stuff
1,000 mg vitamin C
500 mg glutamine
200 mg coenzyme Q10
100 mg DMG (dimethylglycine)
75 mg B-complex vitamin

1. Push the lemon, lime, grapefruit, cucumber, and celery through the juicer.
2. Add the white tea, aloe vera juice, cayenne, Green Stuff, and supplements to the juice mixture, and stir well.
3. Serve immediately.

MAKES 2 SERVINGS.

JAMMIN' YAMS

1 yam, quartered
2 pears, quartered
2 cups strawberries, hulled
1 apple, cored and quartered
1 cup spring water

1. Push the yam, pears, strawberries, and apple through the juicer.
2. Add spring water and stir well.
3. Serve immediately.

MAKES 1 SERVINGS.

JUICE BREAK

POWER 2

1 cucumber, peeled, quartered lengthwise
6 stalks celery
2 medium tomatoes, quartered
1 cup spring water
2 tablespoons vegetable, soy, or rice protein powder (approximately 30 grams)
1/2 teaspoon Gary Null's Green Stuff
pinch cayenne pepper

1. Push the cucumber, celery, and tomatoes through the juicer.
2. In a blender, combine juice mixture, spring water, protein powder, Green Stuff, and cayenne, and blend well.
3. Serve immediately.

MAKES 2 SERVINGS.

JUNIOR JUICE*

3 stalks celery, tops removed, peeled
½ cup cantaloupe, rind removed, cubed
¼ cup pears, cubed
1 cup purified water

1. Push the celery, cantaloupe, and pears through the juicer.
2. Combine the water and juice mixture, and stir well.
3. Refrigerate.
4. Serve over the course of 1–2 days.

MAKES APPROXIMATELY 2 SERVINGS.

*Chef's Note: This is a tasty diluted juice for children. (Diluted juice is easier to digest.)

KIWI-BANANA SHAKE

POWER 2

2 cups soymilk
2 bananas, peeled
2 kiwis, peeled and quartered
¼ teaspoon vanilla extract
¼ teaspoon nutmeg
1 cup ice cubes
3 tablespoons agave or a dash of stevia (optional)

1. Combine the soymilk, bananas, kiwis, vanilla, nutmeg, ice, and sweetener in a blender, and blend until smooth.
2. Serve immediately.

MAKES 2 SERVINGS.

LIFE OF THE PARTY CITRUS PUNCH

POWER 1

12 tangerines or oranges, cubed
4 black or red plums, pitted and halved
3 apricots, pitted and halved
2 grapefruits, cubed
1 lime, quartered
1 lemon, quartered
12 ice cubes

1. Push the tangerines or oranges, plums, apricots, grapefruits, lime, and lemon through the juicer.
2. Stir well.
3. Pour into tall glasses filled with ice.
4. Serve immediately.

MAKES 12 SERVINGS.

LIVER FLUSH

POWER 3

1 cup dandelion greens, chopped
1 guava, peeled, seeded, and quartered
¼ cup burdock root, peeled
1 red pepper, quartered
4 cups celery, chopped
3 tangerines, quartered
1 cup broccoli, chopped
½ cup sweet onion, chopped
1 cup green tea, chilled
10 drops liquid milk thistle
10–20 drops turmeric
dash cayenne

1. Push the greens, guava, burdock root, red pepper, celery, tangerines, broccoli, and onion through the juicer.
2. Add the green tea, liquid milk thistle, turmeric, and cayenne to the juice mixture, and stir well.
3. Serve immediately.

MAKES 2 SERVINGS.

LUSCIOUS BERRIES AND FRENCH CREAM

POWER 2

1 cup blueberries
1 cup blackberries
1 cup cherries, pitted
1 cup strawberries, hulled
1/2 cup cranberries
1 cup coconut milk
1/2 teaspoon vanilla extract
1 tablespoon soy protein powder
1 teaspoon coconut oil
1 cup French vanilla soy creamer

1. In a blender, combine blueberries, blackberries, cherries, strawberries, cranberries, coconut milk, vanilla, protein powder, coconut oil, and soy creamer, and blend until smooth.
2. Serve immediately.

MAKES 2 SERVINGS.

LUSH PECAN SHAKE

POWER   2

1 cup coconut milk
1 cup pecans, halved
1 cup French vanilla soy creamer
3 tablespoons agave or other sweetener
3 tablespoons pure vanilla flavor
3 tablespoons almond nut butter
2 teaspoons pure dark chocolate

1. In a blender, combine coconut milk, pecan halves, soy
   creamer, sweetener, vanilla, almond nut butter, and dark
   chocolate, and blend until smooth.
2. Refrigerate until chilled before serving.

MAKES 2 SERVINGS.

MEAN GREEN HEALING MACHINE

POWER 1

2 cups kale, chopped
1 cup parsley, chopped
1 cup spinach, chopped
4 stalks celery
1/2 cup watercress, chopped
1/2 cup arugula, chopped
2 cups spring water
2 teaspoons Gary Null's Greens & Grains

1. Push kale, parsley, spinach, celery, watercress, and arugula through the juicer.
2. In a blender, combine the spring water, juice mixture, and Greens & Grains powder, and blend until smooth.
3. Serve immediately.

MAKES 2 SERVINGS.

MELLOW MELON

1 1/2 cups honeydew melon, rind removed, cubed
1 1/2 cups cantaloupe, rind removed, cubed
1 cup cassava melon, rind removed, cubed
1 lemon, quartered
2 cups watermelon, rind removed, cubed
1 cup pineapple, peeled and cubed
1/2 teaspoon vitamin C powder

1. Push the honeydew, cantaloupe, cassava, lemon, watermelon, and pineapple through the juicer.
2. In a blender, combine the juice mixture with the vitamin C powder, and blend well.
3. Serve immediately.

MAKES 2 SERVINGS.

MUSCLE BUSTER

POWER 3

1 apple, cored and quartered
1 banana, peeled and frozen
2 scoops soy protein powder
6 tablespoons creamy almond butter
½ cup vanilla soy ice cream
2 teaspoons chia seeds
10–12 ice cubes
2 cups rice milk
1 teaspoon glutamine
1 teaspoon carnitine
300 mg creatine
100 mg coenzyme Q10
10 drops licorice tincture

1. Push the apple through the juicer.
2. In a blender, combine banana, protein powder, almond butter, soy ice cream, chia seeds, and ice cubes, and blend until smooth.
3. Add the apple juice, rice milk, and supplements to the mixture, and blend until well combined.
4. Serve immediately.

MAKES 1 SERVING.

MUSCLE EXPANDER

POWER 2

*2 heaping tablespoons soy protein powder with branched-chain amino
  acids (approximately 30 grams protein)*
1 banana, peeled
¼ teaspoon cinnamon
2 cups rice milk
1,000 mg glutamine powder
500 mg carnitine
1 teaspoon creatine powder

1. In a blender, combine protein powder, banana, cinnamon, rice
   milk, and supplements, and blend until smooth.
2. Serve immediately.

MAKES 1 SERVING.

NICE VEINS

¼ cup cherries or raspberries, pitted
¼ cup lime, peeled and quartered
1 cup purple grapes, with seeds
3 stalks celery
1 parsnip, top removed, sliced lengthwise
2 cups white tea, chilled
4 ounces aloe vera juice
1 teaspoon flaxseed oil
1 cup horse chestnuts
500 mg quercetin
400 IU vitamin E
200 mg coenzyme Q10
200 mg DMG (dimethylglycine)
150 mg ginkgo biloba
30 mg zinc
bromelain, as directed by manufacturer
Butcher's broom, as directed by manufacturer
hawthorn berries, as directed by manufacturer
bilberry, as directed by manufacturer

1. Push cherries or raspberries, lime, grapes, celery, and parsnip through the juicer.
2. In a blender, combine juice mixture with white tea, aloe vera juice, flaxseed oil, horse chestnuts, and supplements, and blend until smooth.
3. Serve immediately.

MAKES 2 SERVINGS.

NOURISHING SKIN SHAKE

7 cucumbers, sliced lengthwise
1 lemon, quartered
1 grapefruit, quartered
1 cup red grapes, with seeds, or 1 teaspoon grape concentrate
1 cup broccoli sprouts, chopped
1 sweet potato, cubed
2 cups green tea, chilled
1 avocado, peeled and pitted
2 tablespoons aloe vera concentrate
2 tablespoons Gary Null's Friendly Fiber
1 tablespoon Gary Null's Green Stuff
1 teaspoon flaxseed oil
1 teaspoon acidophilus
1,000 mg vitamin C
200 mg chromium picolinate
50 mg red clover
15 mg zinc

1. Push the cucumbers, lemon, grapefruit, grapes or grape concentrate, sprouts, and sweet potato through the juicer.
2. In a blender, combine the juice mixture with the green tea, avocado, aloe vera, Friendly Fiber, Green Stuff, flaxseed oil, and supplements, and blend until smooth.
3. Serve immediately.

MAKES 3 SERVINGS.

OCEAN IN A GLASS

POWER 1

2 apples, quartered
2 pears, quartered
1-inch piece gingerroot, peeled
2 cucumbers, sliced lengthwise
4 stalks celery
1 ounce wakame sea vegetable
1 ounce kombu sea vegetable
1 ounce dulse sea vegetable
2 teaspoons Gary Null's Green Stuff

1. Push the apples, pears, ginger, cucumber, celery, and sea vegetables through the juicer.
2. In a blender, combine the juice mixture with the Green Stuff, and blend well.
3. Serve immediately.

MAKES 1 SERVING.

ONE-DAY FASTING JUICE

POWER 1

2 cucumbers, sliced
1 apple, cored and quartered
4 stalks celery
1/2 lemon, halved
1 cup red or purple grapes, with seeds
1 cup watermelon, rind removed, cubed
2 cups green tea, chilled
dash cayenne
2 tablespoons soy protein powder
1 tablespoon Gary Null's Friendly Fiber
1 teaspoon flaxseed oil
1/4 teaspoon turmeric
1,000 mg vitamin C
200 mg green tea
50 mg B-complex vitamin

1. Push the cucumbers, apple, celery, lemon, grapes, and watermelon through the juicer.
2. In a blender, combine the juice mixture with the green tea, cayenne, protein powder, Friendly Fiber, flaxseed oil, turmeric, and supplements, and blend well.
3. Keep refrigerated. Serve 3–4 times throughout the day.

MAKES 3–4 SERVINGS.

PAPAYA-ORANGE PROTEIN SHAKE

POWER 2

2 cups rice milk or soymilk
½ cup papaya, peeled and sliced
1 cup orange juice
1 cup strawberries, hulled
½ teaspoon cinnamon
1 cup ice cubes
1 scoop soy protein powder

1. Combine rice milk or soymilk, papaya, orange juice, strawberries, cinnamon, ice, and protein powder in a blender, and blend until smooth.
2. Serve immediately.

MAKES 2 SERVINGS.

PAPAYA PEAR PERFECT

4 ripe papayas, peeled, seeded, and quartered
3 pears, cored and quartered
1 teaspoon flaxseed oil

1. Push the papayas and pear through the juicer.
2. Add the flaxseed oil to the juice, and stir well.
3. Serve immediately.

MAKES 2 SERVINGS.

PEPPERMINT SHAKE

POWER 2

1 cup dates, chopped
1 cup figs, chopped
1 banana, peeled and frozen
1 cup rice milk or soymilk
1 cup coconut milk
1 bunch fresh mint

1. In a blender, combine dates, figs, and banana with rice milk or soymilk, and coconut milk.
2. Push the mint through the juicer.
3. Drizzle mint juice on top of the blended mixture.
4. Serve chilled.

MAKES 2 SERVINGS.

PEPPERMINT TEA

POWER 1

2 cups purified water
4 peppermint tea bags
4 ounces fresh gingerroot, peeled, cut into 1/2-inch pieces
1 1/2 tablespoons agave or stevia (optional)
1/4 cup lemon juice, freshly squeezed
10 ice cubes
1 large lemon, sliced into 1/4-inch-thick half-moons, as garnish
    (optional)
fresh mint, as garnish (optional)

1. In a small saucepan, combine the water, tea bags, and ginger
   over moderate heat and simmer, covered, for 8–10 minutes,
   or until fully brewed. Stir in the agave or stevia, if desired,
   until well combined, and set aside to cool completely.
2. In a large pitcher, mix the tea, lemon juice, and ice.
3. Stir together until well combined.
4. Pour into glasses and garnish with lemon slices and fresh
   mint, if desired.
5. Serve immediately.

MAKES 10 SERVINGS.

PINEAPPLE-BANANA SURPRISE

POWER 2

3 cups Very Vanilla soymilk
1½ cups pineapple juice
1 banana, peeled
1 scoop soy protein powder (or 1 scoop Gary Null's Muscle with Rice
  Protein)
1½ teaspoons agave or other sweetener

1. In a blender, combine soymilk, pineapple juice, banana,
   protein powder, and sweetener, and blend until smooth.
2. Serve immediately.

MAKES 2 SERVINGS.

PINEAPPLE SPROUT JUICE

2 cups pineapple, peeled, cored, and cubed
½ cup spicy sprouts
½ cup sunflower sprouts
2 cups spring water
½ teaspoon ground cloves

1. Push the pineapple, spicy sprouts, and sunflower sprouts
   through the juicer.
2. Stir the spring water and cloves into the juice mixture.
3. Serve immediately.

MAKES 2 SERVINGS.

PLUM GOOD!

POWER 2

4 red plums, pitted
1 pear, cored, cut into small chunks
1 cup raspberries
1 cup strawberries, hulled
1/2 cup red cabbage, quartered
1/2 cup blueberries
1 tablespoon pomegranate juice concentrate
1 cup red grapes, with seeds
2 cups spring water
1/2 cup ice

1. In a blender, combine plums, pear, raspberries, strawberries, cabbage, blueberries, pomegranate juice concentrate, red grapes, spring water, and ice, and blend until smooth.
2. Serve immediately.

MAKES 2 CUPS.

POTATO SWEET SHAKE

POWER 2

2 sweet potatoes, peeled and cut into 2-inch cubes
4 dates, pitted and halved
2 cups vanilla rice milk or soymilk
2 bananas, peeled and frozen
1 tablespoon pure vanilla extract
2 tablespoons macadamia nut butter
1 teaspoon coconut oil
cinnamon, to taste
12 ice cubes

1. Steam the sweet potatoes until tender, about 10–15 minutes, and then run them under cold water until they are cooled.
2. In a blender, combine sweet potatoes, dates, rice milk or soymilk, bananas, vanilla, macadamia nut butter, coconut oil, and cinnamon, and blend until smooth and creamy.
3. Pour into tall glasses filled with ice.
4. Serve immediately.

MAKES 4 SERVINGS.

POWER JOINTS

POWER 1

1/2 head cabbage, any color, chopped
1/2 cup pineapple, peeled and quartered
1/4 cup broccoli, chopped
1 cup endive, chopped
2 apples, cored and quartered
2 cups green tea, chilled
dash turmeric
bromelain, as directed by manufacturer
500 mg chondroitin sulfate
500 mg glucosamine sulfate
500 mg MSM (methylsulfonylmethane)
500 mg calcium
500 mg magnesium
500 mg vitamin C
400 IU vitamin D
100 mg TMG (trimethylglycine)
50 mg B-complex vitamin
20 mg boswellia
10 mg silica
5 mg boron
3 mg vitamin K

1. Push the cabbage, pineapple, broccoli, endive, and apples through the juicer.
2. In a blender, combine the juice mixture with the green tea, turmeric, and supplements, and blend well.
3. Serve immediately.

MAKES 2 SERVINGS.

POWER MOJO SHAKE

POWER 1

1½ *cups water*
1½ *cups raspberries*
1¼ *cups apple juice*
1¼ *cups kiwi juice*
2 *cups rice milk*
4 *tablespoons soy protein powder*
2 *tablespoons cherry concentrate*
1½ *teaspoons carob powder*
½ *cup ice cubes*

1. In a blender, combine water, raspberries, apple juice, kiwi juice, rice milk, protein powder, cherry concentrate, carob powder, and ice cubes, and blend until smooth.
2. Serve immediately.

MAKES 2 SERVINGS.

PRE-EXERCISE POWER DRINK

POWER 3

1 cup watermelon, rind removed, cut into 2-inch pieces
2 large tangerines, quartered
1 lime, quartered
1 cup blueberries
2 tablespoons soy or rice protein powder
1 tablespoon Gary Null's Green Stuff
1 tablespoon Gary Null's Red Stuff
200 mg coenzyme Q10
500 mg L-carnitine
400 IU vitamin E
500 mg glutamine

1. Push the watermelon, tangerines, lime, and blueberries through the juicer.
2. In a blender, combine the juice mixture, protein powder, Green Stuff, Red Stuff, and supplements, and blend well.
3. Serve immediately.

MAKES 8 SERVINGS.

REAL GINGER ALE

POWER 2

1-inch section gingerroot, peeled
2 cups watermelon, with rind, cubed
1 pint red grapes, with seeds
1 medium tangerine, quartered
4 ounces sparkling mineral water

1. Push gingerroot, watermelon, red grapes, and tangerine through the juicer.
2. Add the mineral water to the juice mixture and stir well.
3. Serve immediately.

MAKES 2 SERVINGS.

RED AND YELLOW PEPPER APPLE JUICE

POWER 1

2 yellow peppers, cored, stems and seeds removed
2 red peppers, cored, stems and seeds removed
2 apples, cored and quartered

1. Push the peppers and apples through the juicer.
2. Stir well.
3. Serve immediately.

MAKES 1 SERVING.

REFRESHING GUAVA

POWER 1

1 papaya, peeled and pitted
2 medium guavas, peeled, seeded, and quartered lengthwise
2 cucumbers, quartered lengthwise
1 tangerine, quartered

1. Push papaya, guavas, cucumbers, and tangerine through the juicer.
2. Stir well.
3. Serve immediately.

MAKES 1 SERVING.

REVITALIZER JUICE

POWER 1

1 cup strawberries, hulled and halved
1 cup blueberries
1 pineapple, rind removed, cubed
1 ounce pomegranate concentrate
1 ounce papaya concentrate
1 ounce cranberry concentrate

1. Push the strawberries, blueberries, and pineapple through the juicer.
2. Add the pomegranate, papaya, and cranberry concentrates to the juice mixture, and stir well.
3. Serve immediately.

MAKES 1 SERVING.

RISE AND SHINE

POWER 2

1 cup blueberries
1 cup blackberries
2 tablespoons soy protein powder
1 tablespoon Gary Null's Red Stuff
1 tablespoon Gary Null's Green Stuff
2 teaspoons black cherry concentrate
2 teaspoons pomegranate concentrate
2 teaspoons papaya concentrate
2 teaspoons mango concentrate
2 teaspoons grape concentrate
1 teaspoon flaxseed oil
1,000 mg vitamin C
200 mg coenzyme Q10
500 mg carnosine
500 mg carnitine
200 mg green tea
50 mg B-complex vitamin

1. In a blender, combine blueberries, blackberries, protein powder, Red Stuff, Green Stuff, black cherry, pomegranate, papaya, mango, and grape concentrates, flaxseed oil, and supplements, and blend well.
2. Serve immediately.

MAKES 1 SERVING.

ROOTS JUICE

POWER 2

4 burdock roots, sliced
1 parsnip, top removed, sliced
1 radish
1 carrot, top removed, sliced lengthwise
1 yam, sliced lengthwise
1 cup parsley greens, chopped
3 teaspoons agave syrup or stevia (optional)

1. Push the burdock, parsnip, radish, carrot, yam, and parsley greens through the juicer.
2. In a blender, combine the juice mixture with agave, if desired, and blend well.
3. Serve immediately.

MAKES 2 SERVINGS.

SEAWEED JUICE

POWER 1

1 ounce wakame sea vegetable, cut in small pieces
1 ounce kombu sea vegetable, cut in small pieces
1 ounce hijiki sea vegetable, cut in small pieces
1 cup arugula, chopped
6 stalks celery
2 apples, cored and quartered
1 cup pineapple, rind removed, cubed

1. In a blender or food processor, chop the sea vegetables until very fine.
2. Push the arugula, celery, apples, and pineapple through the juicer.
3. Add the sea vegetables to the juice mixture and stir well.
4. Serve immediately.

MAKES 1 SERVING.

SKIN CARE

POWER 1

1 cup asparagus, sliced
1 cup cucumbers, sliced
1 cup green olives, pitted
1 cup watercress, chopped
2 ounces parsley, chopped
1 apple, cored and quartered
4 parsnips, tops removed, sliced lengthwise
1 lemon, quartered
1 lime, quartered
2 ounces aloe vera juice
1 teaspoon coconut oil
1 teaspoon flaxseed oil

1. Push the asparagus, cucumbers, green olives, watercress, parsley, apple, parsnips, lemon, and lime through the juicer.
2. Add the aloe vera juice, coconut oil, and flaxseed oil to the juice mixture, and stir well.
3. Serve immediately.

MAKES 1 SERVING.

SKIN ELIXIR

1 medium cucumber, cut in slices
3 parsnips, tops removed, cubed
1 pineapple, rind removed, cubed
1 lemon, quartered
1 ounce aloe vera
1 teaspoon flaxseed oil
1 teaspoon coconut oil
200 mg white or green tea
1,000 mg vitamin C
400 IU vitamin E

1. Push the cucumber, parsnips, pineapple, and lemon through the juicer.
2. Mix in the aloe vera, flaxseed oil, coconut oil, tea, and supplements, and stir well.
3. Serve immediately.

MAKES 5 SERVINGS.

SMART JUICE

POWER 1

2 cups Swiss chard, chopped
1½ cups avocado, peeled and pitted
½ head cabbage, shredded
1 cup watercress, chopped
3 apples, quartered
2 peaches, quartered and pitted
2 black plums, pitted
200 IU vitamin E
125 mg ginkgo biloba
100 mg ginseng
100 mg glutamine
100 mg phosphatidylserine
500 mcg vitamin B$_{12}$
100 mg DHA (docosahexaenoic acid)
25 mg B-complex vitamin

1. Push the Swiss chard, avocado, cabbage, watercress, apples, peaches, and plums through the juicer.
2. In a blender, combine the juice mixture with the supplements and blend well.
3. Serve immediately.

MAKES 3 SERVINGS.

SMOOTH NUTS SHAKE

POWER 3

2 cups vanilla rice milk or soymilk
1 pint cherries, pitted
1 cup apple juice
1 banana, peeled and frozen
4 tablespoons almond butter
4 tablespoons macadamia nut butter
4 tablespoons sesame butter
4 tablespoons walnut butter

1. In a blender or food processor, combine rice milk or soymilk, cherries, apple juice, and banana, and blend well.
2. Add the butters to the blended mixture and blend until smooth.
3. Serve immediately.

MAKES 3 SERVINGS.

SOUND SLEEP

POWER 3

1 pear, quartered
4 stalks celery
1 cucumber, quartered
2-inch piece gingerroot, peeled
1/2 head cabbage, any color, chopped
2 bananas, peeled
100 mg valerian root
1,000 mg calcium
1,000 mg magnesium
200 mg threonine
3 mg melatonin

1. Push the pear, celery, cucumber, ginger, and cabbage through the juicer.
2. In a blender, combine the juice mixture, bananas, and supplements, and blend until smooth.
3. Serve immediately.

MAKES 3 SERVINGS.

SPEARMINT WATERMELON COOLER

POWER 1

8 cups purified water
6 spearmint tea bags
1 watermelon, rind removed, cubed
2 tangerines, quartered
2 lemons, quartered
10 ice cubes
1 large lemon, sliced into ¼-inch-thick half-moons, as garnish (optional)
fresh mint, as garnish (optional)

1. In a small saucepan, combine the water and tea bags over moderate heat and simmer, covered, for 8–10 minutes, or until fully brewed. Set aside and allow to cool completely.
2. Push the melon, tangerines, and lemons through the juicer.
3. In a large pitcher, combine the juice mixture, tea, and ice, and stir together until well blended.
4. Pour into glasses and garnish with lemon slices and mint, if desired.
5. Serve immediately.

MAKES 8 SERVINGS.

SPICY POTATO TOMATO

POWER 1

2 medium tomatoes, quartered
1 potato, quartered
4 stalks celery
½ cup radishes
dash cayenne

1. Push tomatoes, potato, celery, and radishes through the juicer. Add the cayenne and mix well.
2. Serve immediately.

MAKES 1 SERVING.

SPRING CLEANING

POWER 5

6–7 stalks celery
1 carrot, top removed, sliced lengthwise
2 cucumbers, sliced lengthwise
1 beet, quartered
1 lemon, quartered
3 cloves garlic, peeled
1/2 sweet onion, peeled and quartered
1 bunch fresh basil
1 small bunch lemongrass
1-inch piece gingerroot, peeled
1/2 cabbage, quartered
1 teaspoon flaxseed oil
1 teaspoon coconut oil
20 drops cat's claw

1. Push celery, carrot, cucumbers, beet, lemon, garlic, onion, basil, lemongrass, gingerroot, and cabbage through the juicer.
2. Add the flaxseed and coconut oils and cat's claw to the juice mixture, and stir well.
3. Serve immediately.

MAKES 3 SERVINGS.

STOMACH ACID BUSTER

POWER 3

8 stalks celery, top leaves removed
1 head cabbage, sliced
2-inch piece gingerroot, peeled
$1/2$ cup blueberries
1 apple, cored and quartered
4 ounces aloe vera concentrate
$1/2$ teaspoon turmeric
$1/2$ teaspoon fennel seed
$1/2$ teaspoon anise
2 teaspoons acidophilus
1,000 mg glutamine
1,000 mg vitamin C
500 mg quercetin
300 mg green tea
600 IU vitamin E
300 mg coenzyme Q10
500 mg magnesium
1,000 mg omega-3
artichoke leaf extract, as directed by manufacturer
digestive enzymes, as directed by manufacturer
4 ounces sparkling water

1. Use the celery stalks to push the cabbage and gingerroot
   through the juicer, juicing the celery in the process. Set aside.
2. Push the blueberries and apple through the juicer.
3. Combine juices and stir well.
4. In a blender, combine the juice mixture and aloe vera
   concentrate, turmeric, fennel seed, anise, and supplements,
   and blend until smooth.
5. Top with sparkling water.
6. Serve immediately.

MAKES 2 SERVINGS.

STRONG HEART

POWER 3

5 cloves garlic, peeled
1 medium artichoke heart
1½ cups cabbage, any color,
   chopped
½ pint green beans, tops removed
1 cup alfalfa sprouts
4 stalks celery
2 cucumbers, sliced lengthwise
½ teaspoon turmeric
1,000 mg vitamin C
500 mg magnesium
500 mg calcium
500 mg L-carnitine
300 mg coenzyme Q10
300 mg green tea
200 mg alpha-lipoic acid

150 mg ginkgo biloba
100 mg potassium
100 mg TMG
   (tri-methyl-glycine)
100 mg grape seed extract
50 mg B-complex vitamin
10 mg polycosanol
400 IU vitamin E
5 mg vitamin K
3 mg melatonin
SAMe, as directed by
   manufacturer
L-arginine, as directed by
   manufacturer
IPS (iron protein succinylate), as
   directed by manufacturer

1. Push the garlic, artichoke, cabbage, green beans, alfalfa
   sprouts, celery, and cucumbers through the juicer.
2. Add the turmeric and the supplements to the juice mixture,
   and stir well.
3. Serve immediately.

MAKES 3 SERVINGS.

SUNRISE LYCOPENE COCKTAIL

POWER 4

1 large bunch flat-leaf parsley (about ½ pound)
2 cucumbers, sliced lengthwise
3 large tomatoes, cored and quartered
3 stalks celery
3 red peppers, quartered
3 radishes
2 cloves garlic, peeled
⅓ red onion
sea salt, to taste
1 teaspoon green vegetable powder
dash cayenne (optional)
12 ice cubes
4 stalks celery, as garnish (optional)

1. Bunch up the parsley and push through the juicer, alternating it with the cucumbers, tomatoes, celery, peppers, radishes, garlic, and onion.
2. Add the salt, vegetable powder, and cayenne to the mixture, and stir well.
3. Pour into tall glasses filled with ice, and garnish with celery stalks, if desired.
4. Serve immediately.

MAKES 4 SERVINGS.

SUPER ANTIOXIDANT JUICE

POWER 1

1 cup wolfberries
1 cup red grapes, with seeds
1/2 medium watermelon, rind removed, cubed
1/2 cup broccoli, chopped
1 cup collard greens, ends cut, chopped
1 cup spinach, ends cut, chopped
3 parsnips, tops removed, quartered
500 mg vitamin C
200 IU vitamin E
15 mg zinc
100 mg quercetin
20 mg lycopene
50 mg tocotrienols
200 mg citrus bioflavonoids
25 mg bilberry extract
100 mg grape seed extract
200 mg green tea
50 mg coenzyme Q10
100 mg NAC (N-acetylcysteine)
25 mg lutein

1. Push the wolfberries, red grapes, watermelon, broccoli, collard greens, spinach, and parsnips through the juicer.
2. In a blender, combine the juice mixture with the supplements, and blend well.
3. Serve immediately.

MAKES 4 SERVINGS.

SUPER IMMUNE PUSH

POWER 3

2 medium cloves garlic, peeled
½ cup sweet onion, peeled and
   quartered
1½ cups black or green olives,
   pitted
4 medium tangerines, quartered
1 cup broccoli sprouts
3 apples, cored and quartered
½ lemon, quartered
2 tablespoons agave or other
   sweetener
1 teaspoon coconut oil
1 teaspoon flaxseed oil
3 ounces aloe vera juice
5 drops oregano tincture
20 drops echinacea tincture

20 drops astragalus tincture
10,000 IU vitamin A
1,000 mg vitamin C
200 mg quercetin
100 mg resveratrol
100 mg coenzyme Q10
100 mg grape seed extract
25 mg milk thistle
20 mg astaxanthin
20 mg lycopene
20 mg cat's claw
20 mg red clover
10 mg zinc
200 mg Beta 1, 3-D-glucan
10–20 drops goldenseal (optional)

1. Push the garlic, onion, olives, tangerines, broccoli sprouts,
   apples, and lemon through the juicer.
2. In a blender, combine the juice mixture, the agave, coconut and
   flaxseed oils, aloe vera juice, and supplements, and blend well.
3. Serve immediately.

MAKES 2 SERVINGS.

SWEET BREATH

1 cup fresh peppermint leaf, chopped
5 stalks celery
1/2 cup fresh parsley, chopped
1 teaspoon fennel
1 teaspoon whole anise seed

1. Push the peppermint, celery, and parsley through the juicer.
2. Stir in the fennel and anise, and mix well.
3. Serve immediately.

MAKES 1 SERVING.

SWEET CUCUMBER COOLER

POWER 1

3 cucumbers, quartered lengthwise
2 cups red grapes, with seeds
1 lemon, quartered
1-inch piece gingerroot, peeled

1. Push the cucumbers, grapes, lemon, and gingerroot through the juicer.
2. Stir well.
3. Serve immediately.

MAKES 2 SERVINGS.

SWEET DANDELION

POWER 3

2 apples, cored and quartered
4 cups honeydew melon, rind removed, cubed
1 cup cherries, pitted
1 cup dandelion greens, chopped
1 cup broccoli, chopped
1 cup tomato, chopped
1-inch piece gingerroot, peeled
1 tablespoon agave or other sweetener

1. Push the apples, melon, cherries, dandelion greens, broccoli, tomato, and gingerroot through the juicer.
2. Add sweetener to the juice mixture and stir well.
3. Chill before serving.

MAKES 2 SERVINGS.

SWEET POTATO, CUCUMBER, AND KIWI

2 cucumbers, sliced
4 kiwis, peeled and quartered
1 sweet potato, peeled and quartered
2 teaspoons agave or other sweetener
1 teaspoon pomegranate concentrate
6 ice cubes

1. Push the cucumbers, kiwis, and sweet potato through the juicer.
2. In a blender, combine the juice mixture, sweetener, and pomegranate concentrate, and blend well.
3. Pour into a tall glass filled with ice.
4. Serve immediately.

MAKES 1 SERVING.

THE DEEP CLEANSE

POWER 3

2 apples, cored and quartered
3 stalks celery
1 grapefruit, peeled and quartered
1 lemon, quartered
1 lime, quartered
1/2 cup cabbage, chopped
1/2 clove garlic, peeled
1 tablespoon ginger, peeled
2 ounces wheatgrass juice*
2 tablespoons Gary Null's Friendly Fiber Powder
1/2 teaspoon turmeric
1 teaspoon flaxseed oil
pinch cayenne pepper

1. Push apples, celery, grapefruit, lemon, lime, cabbage, garlic, and ginger through the juicer.
2. In a blender, combine the juice mixture with wheatgrass juice, Friendly Fiber, turmeric, flaxseed oil, and cayenne pepper, and blend well.
3. Serve immediately.

MAKES 2 SERVINGS.

*Chef's Note: Wheatgrass can be juiced by using a special wheatgrass press. You can also make wheatgrass juice by squeezing the grass into clusters with your hands and juicing these clusters through a traditional fruit and vegetable juicer. If your juicer can't process wheatgrass, you can buy wheatgrass in powder form. One teaspoon of the powder is equal to 2 ounces of fresh wheatgrass.

THE MORNING RUSH JUICE

POWER 2

1 watermelon, with rind, cubed
2 kiwis, skin removed
1 grapefruit, quartered
1 lime, quartered
1 lemon, quartered
1 cucumber, sliced lengthwise
1/2 cup cranberries
1-inch burdock root
2-inch piece ginger, peeled
1/2 cup dandelion greens, chopped
dash turmeric
1,000 mg vitamin C
1,000 mg glutamine
400 IU vitamin E
200 mg white or green tea capsules
100 mg quercetin

1. Push the watermelon, kiwis, grapefruit, lime, lemon, cucumber, cranberries, burdock root, ginger, and dandelion greens through the juicer.
2. In a blender, combine the juice mixture, turmeric, and the supplements, and blend well.
3. Serve immediately.

MAKES 10 SERVINGS.

THE SUPREME ANTIOXIDANT SMOOTHIE

POWER 2

2 cups pineapple, peeled, cored, and cut into 1-inch cubes
1 cup blueberries
8 stalks celery
1 cup pomegranate juice
1 cup unsweetened cranberry juice
1 tablespoon soy protein powder
1 teaspoon Gary Null's Red Stuff
2,000 mg isoflavone genistein
1,000 mg vitamin C powder
400 IU vitamin E
300 mg citrus bioflavonoids
200 mg green tea capsule
100 mg grape seed extract
50 mg coenzyme Q10
25 mg milk thistle
10 mg zinc
10 ice cubes

1. Push the pineapple, blueberries, and celery through the juicer.
2. In a blender, combine the juice mixture with the pomegranate and cranberry juices, and mix well.
3. Add the soy protein powder, Red Stuff, other supplements, and ice, and blend until smooth.
4. Serve immediately.

MAKES 4 SERVINGS.

THE WORKS

POWER 5

½ pound parsnips, tops removed, quartered
1 cup arugula, chopped
1 cup kale, chopped
½ cup wolfberries or blueberries
½ cup Swiss chard, chopped
½ papaya, cubed
2 cloves garlic, peeled
½-inch piece gingerroot, peeled
2 tablespoons soy protein powder
1 tablespoon chia seeds
1 tablespoon cranberry extract
⅛ teaspoon turmeric

1. Push the parsnips, arugula, kale, berries, Swiss chard, papaya, garlic, and gingerroot through the juicer.
2. In a blender, combine the juice mixture, protein powder, chia seeds, cranberry extract, and turmeric, and blend well.
3. Serve immediately.

MAKES 2 SERVINGS.

THIRST BUSTER

4-pound watermelon, rind removed, cut into 1-inch cubes
2¹/₂-pound (large) pineapple, peeled, cored, and cut into 1-inch cubes
6 lemons, quartered
1 cup strawberries, hulled
1 cup raspberries
1 cup cherries, pitted
20–24 ice cubes
1 large orange, sliced into ¹/₄-inch-thick half-moons, as garnish
   (optional)

1. Push watermelon, pineapple, and lemons through the juicer.
2. In a blender combine the juice mixture, berries, and cherries, and blend well.
3. Pour into tall glasses filled with ice and garnish with orange slices, if desired.
4. Serve immediately.

MAKES 4 CUPS.

ULTIMATE DETOX

POWER 2

4 plums, pitted, halved
1/2 cup blueberries
2 stalks celery
1 pear, cored and quartered
1 cup blackberries
1 cup watercress, chopped
2 apples, cored and quartered
2 ounces Jerusalem artichokes
2 ounces aloe vera concentrate
3 tablespoons agave or other sweetener
2 tablespoons Gary Null's Friendly Fiber
2 teaspoons dark cherry concentrate
2 teaspoons pomegranate concentrate
pinch sea vegetables
1 teaspoon acidophilus
1,000 mg vitamin C

1. Push the plums, blueberries, celery, pear, blackberries, watercress, apples, and Jerusalem artichokes through the juicer.
2. In a blender, combine the juice mixture with the aloe vera, agave, Friendly Fiber, cherry and pomegranate concentrates, sea vegetables, and supplements, and blend until smooth.
3. Serve immediately.

MAKES 4 SERVINGS.

VERY BERRY SMOOTHIE

POWER 3

2 cups blueberries
2 cups raspberries
1 cup blackberries
2 cups strawberries, hulled
1 banana, peeled
1 tablespoon soy protein powder
2 cups aloe vera juice
2 cups French vanilla soy creamer
1 teaspoon pomegranate concentrate
1 teaspoon cherry concentrate
1 tablespoon powdered vitamin C complex with quercetin
1 teaspoon flaxseed oil
1 teaspoon Gary Null's Red Stuff

1. In a blender, combine the blueberries, raspberries, blackberries, strawberries, banana, protein powder, aloe vera juice, soy creamer, pomegranate and cherry concentrates, and supplements, and blend until smooth and creamy.
2. Serve immediately.

MAKES 2 SERVINGS.

YANG BANG

POWER 1

2 apples, cored and quartered
2 pears, cored and quartered
1-inch piece gingerroot, peeled and grated
100 mg yohimbe powder
100 mg ginseng
350 mg mura puma
300 mg chrysin
150 mg maca
150 mg nettle
50 mg damiana
dash cayenne

1. Push the apples, pears, and ginger through the juicer.
2. In a blender, combine the juice mixture with the supplements and cayenne, and blend well.
3. Serve immediately.

MAKES 1 SERVING.

YIN AND YANG WATERMELON JUICE

POWER 1

1-inch piece gingerroot, peeled
1 watermelon, rind removed, cubed
1 lemon, quartered
1 cup parsley

1. Push the gingerroot, watermelon, lemon, and parsley through the juicer.
2. Stir well.
3. Serve immediately.

MAKES 3 SERVINGS.

YUMMY IN THE TUMMY

POWER 2

1 cup watermelon, rind removed, cubed
1 medium papaya, peeled, pitted, and cubed
1 medium mango, peeled, pitted, and quartered
1 medium pear, cored and quartered
1 cup red or purple grapes, with seeds
1 bunch kale, chopped
1 cup collard greens, chopped
1 cup dandelion greens, chopped
1 medium zucchini, sliced lengthwise
1 red pepper, quartered
1 teaspoon cinnamon

1. Push the watermelon, papaya, mango, pear, grapes, kale, collard greens, dandelion greens, zucchini, and pepper through the juicer.
2. In a blender, combine the juice mixture with the cinnamon and blend well.
3. Serve immediately.

MAKES 2 SERVINGS.

YUMMY PAPAYA SHAKE

POWER 2

2 cups soymilk
1 cup papaya, chopped
1 banana, peeled
1 cup pineapple chunks, drained
1 teaspoon lemon extract
1 cup ice cubes
1 tablespoon soy protein powder
1 teaspoon flaxseed oil

1. In a blender, combine the soymilk, papaya, banana, pineapple, lemon extract, ice cubes, protein powder, and flaxseed oil, and blend until smooth.
2. Serve immediately.

MAKES 2 SERVINGS.

Chapter Four

BREAKFAST DISHES

AMISH AMARANTH

POWER 1

1 cup amaranth, cooked
1 tablespoon agave or other sweetener
pinch nutmeg
¹/₂ cup peaches, cut into bite-size pieces
pinch allspice

1. Combine amaranth, agave, nutmeg, peaches, and allspice. Mix well.*
2. Serve immediately.

MAKES 1 SERVING.

*Chef's Note: If desired, add rice, soy-, or almond milk to taste and for preferred consistency.

APPLE FRENCH TOAST
WITH BANANA SAUCE

POWER 2

1 cup rice milk or soymilk
1/2 cup applesauce
1 teaspoon cinnamon
1 teaspoon vanilla extract
2 tablespoons egg replacer
4 slices date nut Essene bread
3 tablespoons coconut oil, macadamia nut oil, or mustard seed oil
3 bananas, peeled, puréed
1/3 cup pure maple syrup
1/4 cup walnuts, chopped

1. In a medium-size bowl, combine the rice milk or soymilk, applesauce, cinnamon, vanilla, and egg replacer, and mix with a whisk or fork.
2. Soak the bread on both sides in the mixture.
3. In a skillet, heat the oil over medium heat. Fry bread until light brown on both sides.
4. Top with banana purée, syrup, and nuts.
5. Serve hot.

MAKES 2 SERVINGS.

BERRY BULGUR

POWER 4

1¼ cups rice milk or soymilk
2 tablespoons dried tart cherries
¼ cup whole almonds
¼ cup strawberries, hulled
¼ cup raspberries
¼ cup blueberries
¼ cup blackberries
2 cups bulgur, cooked
3 tablespoons agave or other sweetener
⅛ teaspoon cinnamon or nutmeg
1 teaspoon vanilla or orange extract

1. In a medium-size saucepan, combine the rice milk or soymilk, dried cherries, almonds, and all of the berries, and cook over low heat for 1–2 minutes.
2. Add the bulgur, agave, cinnamon or nutmeg, and vanilla or orange extract, and cook for an additional 1–2 minutes.
3. Mix well.*
4. Serve hot or cold.

MAKES 2 SERVINGS.

Chef's Note: If desired, add rice, soy-, or almond milk to taste and for preferred consistency.

BLUEBERRY-APRICOT OATMEAL

POWER 3

1 cup water
¾ cup rolled oats
½ cup apricot nectar or apple-apricot juice
½ cup blueberries, fresh or frozen
2 tablespoons rice protein powder or soy protein powder
1½–2 tablespoons pure maple syrup (optional)
½ teaspoon cinnamon

1. In a medium-size saucepan, combine water, oats, apricot nectar or juice, blueberries, rice or soy protein powder, maple syrup, if desired, and cinnamon.
2. Cook over medium heat for 8–10 minutes, or until liquid is absorbed.*
3. Serve hot.

MAKES 2 SERVINGS.

Chef's Note: If desired, add rice, soy-, or almond milk to taste and for preferred consistency.

BLUEBERRY SPELT PANCAKES

POWER 3

1/2 cup whole spelt flour
1 teaspoon baking powder
1 teaspoon baking soda
dash ground nutmeg
1 cup plain soy yogurt
1/2 cup bananas, thinly sliced
3/4 cup blueberries, fresh or frozen
3/4 cup macadamia nut oil

1. Preheat oven to 300°F.
2. In a medium-size mixing bowl, combine the flour, baking powder, baking soda, and nutmeg, and mix well with a fork to remove lumps.
3. Add the yogurt, bananas, and blueberries, and mix well.
4. In a large skillet, heat the oil over medium heat.
5. Each cake will require 3–4 tablespoons of batter. Pour the batter into the skillet and cook for 2–3 minutes on each side, until light brown.
6. Keep pancakes warm in oven as you finish preparing the remaining cakes.
7. Serve hot.

MAKES 12 PANCAKES.

CAROB-BLUEBERRY QUINOA

POWER 3

2 cups quinoa, cooked
1 cup blueberries, fresh or frozen
1/2 cup walnuts, chopped
1/4 cup agave or other sweetener
2 tablespoons carob powder
1 tablespoon soy protein powder
1 teaspoon nutmeg, ground

1. In a medium-size saucepan, combine quinoa, blueberries, walnuts, agave, carob powder, soy protein powder, and nutmeg.
2. Cook over low heat for 2–3 minutes.
3. Stir well.*
4. Serve hot.

MAKES 2 SERVINGS.

Chef's Note: If desired, add rice, soy-, or almond milk to taste and for preferred consistency.

CHEWY MUNCHY GRANOLA

POWER 3

2 large carrots (¹/₂ cup pulp), tops removed, sliced lengthwise
1 cup rolled oats
³/₄ cup whole unsalted slivered almonds
¹/₂ cup agave or other sweetener
¹/₄ cup raisins
¹/₈ cup unsulfured molasses
2 tablespoons cherry concentrate
2 tablespoons arrowroot powder
2 teaspoons almond extract
³/₄ teaspoon cinnamon
¹/₄ teaspoon fennel seed

1. Preheat oven to 375°F.
2. Push the carrots through the juicer, and set aside ½ cup of the pulp.
3. In a large mixing bowl, combine the carrot pulp with oats, almonds, agave, raisins, molasses, cherry concentrate, arrowroot powder, almond extract, cinnamon, and fennel seed, and mix well.
4. Spread the mixture on a greased cookie sheet, and bake for 15 minutes, or until the top of the mixture turns brown.
5. Let set in refrigerator for 1 hour before serving.

MAKES 2 SERVINGS.

COCOA KASHA WITH BLUEBERRIES

POWER 3

2 cups cantaloupe, rind removed, cut into pieces (1 cup juice)
1 cup purified water
2½ cups unsweetened rice milk or soymilk
½ cup kasha
½ cup blueberries
¼ cup agave or other sweetener
½ tablespoon pure unsweetened cocoa powder (unsweetened carob
*   powder may be substituted)*
dash cinnamon
dash salt

1. Push the cantaloupe through the juicer. Set aside 1 cup of the juice.
2. In a medium-size saucepan, combine the cantaloupe juice, water, and ½ cup of rice milk or soymilk, and bring to a boil over high heat.
3. Reduce the heat to medium-low, and stir in the kasha. Cook, uncovered, for 3–4 minutes, stirring occasionally.
4. Add the blueberries, agave, cocoa powder, cinnamon, and salt, and cook for an additional 3–4 minutes, stirring occasionally.
5. Serve hot with remaining unsweetened rice milk or soymilk.

MAKES 2 SERVINGS.

COCONUT-BERRY MILLET

POWER 4

1¹/₄ cups coconut milk
2 tablespoons dried tart cherries
2 tablespoons dried cranberries
¹/₂ teaspoon vanilla extract
2 tablespoons sunflower seeds
¹/₄ cup banana, peeled and sliced
¹/₂ teaspoon nutmeg, ground
¹/₄ cup toasted coconut, shredded
3 cups millet, cooked
1 tablespoon soy protein powder
2 tablespoons carob powder
1¹/₂ tablespoons coconut oil
3 tablespoons almonds, chopped

1. In a medium-size saucepan, combine the milk, cherries, dried berries, and vanilla, and bring to a simmer over low heat.
2. Add the sunflower seeds, banana, nutmeg, coconut, cooked millet, protein powder, carob powder, coconut oil, and chopped almonds, and stir well.
3. Cook an additional 1–2 minutes.*
4. Serve either hot or cold.

MAKES 2 SERVINGS.

Chef's Note: If desired, add rice, soy-, or almond milk to taste and for preferred consistency.

CREAMY BANANA-FIG AMARANTH

POWER 2

1 cup amaranth, cooked
1 banana, mashed
2 tablespoons carob chips
2 tablespoons cashews
2 figs, chopped

1. Combine amaranth, banana, carob chips, cashews, and figs.
2. Mix well.*
3. Serve immediately.

MAKES 2 SERVINGS.

Chef's Note: If desired, add rice, soy-, or almond milk to taste and for preferred consistency.

CREAMY CAROB-COCONUT AMARANTH

POWER 2

1¹/4 cups coconut milk
2 tablespoons raisins
¹/2 teaspoon vanilla extract
3 cups amaranth, cooked
2 tablespoons carob powder
2 tablespoons walnuts, chopped
2 tablespoons sunflower seeds
¹/4 cup banana, sliced
¹/2 teaspoon nutmeg, ground
¹/4 cup toasted coconut, shredded

1. In a medium-size saucepan, combine the milk, raisins, and
   vanilla, and bring to a simmer over low heat.
2. Stir in the cooked amaranth, carob powder, walnuts,
   sunflower seeds, banana, nutmeg, and shredded coconut.
3. Cook for another 1–2 minutes.*
4. Serve either hot or cold.

MAKES 2 SERVINGS.

Chef's Note: If desired, add rice, soy-, or almond milk to taste and for preferred consistency.

HAWAIIAN COCONUT BUCKWHEAT CEREAL

POWER 2

1/3 cup cream of buckwheat, uncooked
3/4 cup water
1/2 cup banana, mashed
1/4 cup coconut flakes
3 tablespoons raisins
1/4 cup oat germ (optional)
2–3 tablespoons pure maple syrup
1 1/2 teaspoons cinnamon, ground
2 cups soymilk or piña colada juice

1. In a medium-size saucepan, combine the buckwheat and water, and bring to a boil over medium heat.
2. Cook 3–7 minutes.
3. Stir in the banana, coconut, raisins, oat germ, maple syrup, and cinnamon, and cook another 1–2 minutes.
4. Serve with soymilk or piña colada juice on top.

MAKES 2 SERVINGS.

IT'S NICE WITH RICE

POWER 1

1 cup brown rice, cooked (room temperature)
2 tablespoons dried apricots, chopped
2 tablespoons almond, chopped
3 tablespoons unsweetened coconut, shredded
1/4 cup water
1 tablespoon sunflower seeds

1. Mix together brown rice, apricots, almond, and coconut.
2. In a blender or food processor, purée half the mixture with 1/4 cup of water, until coarsely ground.
3. Add purée back into the rest of the rice mixture.
4. Sprinkle with sunflower seeds and mix well.*
5. Serve immediately.

MAKES 1 SERVING.

Chef's Note: If desired, add rice, soy-, or almond milk to taste and for preferred consistency.

MAGIC MILLET

POWER 2

4 cups pineapple, peeled and cubed (approximately 1½ cups juice)
1 cup purified water
½ cup millet
¼ cup banana, mashed
3 tablespoons unsweetened coconut, flaked
2 tablespoons dates, chopped
½ teaspoon pure almond extract
2 cups unsweetened rice milk, soymilk, or juice

1. Push the pineapple through the juicer.
2. In a large saucepan, combine the pineapple juice and water, and bring to a boil over high heat, approximately 10 minutes.
3. Reduce the heat to medium-low, and stir in the millet. Cook, uncovered, until the water is absorbed, about 45 minutes.
4. Add the banana, coconut, dates, and almond extract, and stir occasionally, until all liquid is absorbed.
5. Serve hot with unsweetened rice milk, soymilk, or juice.

MAKES 2 SERVINGS.

MILLET ALMOND CINNAMON

POWER 2

1 cup millet
2 cups purified water
1/2 cup fresh pineapple, peeled and diced
2 tablespoons almonds, blanched and chopped
pinch cinnamon

1. In a saucepan, combine millet with water, and bring to a boil over medium heat.
2. Lower heat and cook, stirring occasionally, until water is absorbed.
3. Add the pineapple, almonds, and cinnamon, and mix well.*
4. Serve hot or cold.

MAKES 2 SERVINGS.

*__Chef's Note:__ If desired, add rice, soy-, or almond milk to taste and for preferred consistency.

ORANGE-GLAZED APPLES WITH QUINOA

POWER 3

2 large Fuji or Red Delicious apples
1/4 cup maple syrup
1/4 cup orange juice
2 tablespoons orange zest, grated
1/2 tablespoon olive oil
1/2 tablespoon cinnamon
1 cup quinoa, cooked
1 kiwi, sliced lengthwise
dollop soy vanilla yogurt
6 red raspberries

1. Core and slice apples into 12 slices. Set aside.
2. In a saucepan, combine the maple syrup, orange juice, orange zest, oil, and cinnamon. Simmer for 10 minutes.
3. Add the apples to the glaze, making sure to coat them well. Cook, covered, for 8 minutes.
4. Spoon apples over cooked quinoa, garnish with kiwi slices, and top with a dollop of soy vanilla yogurt and raspberries.
5. Serve immediately.

MAKES 4 SERVINGS.

ORANGE MAPLE MARMALADE

POWER 1

3/4 cup orange juice
2 tablespoons pure maple syrup
2 tablespoons agave or other sweetener
1 teaspoon guar gum
1 1/2 teaspoons orange rind, grated

1. In a medium-size saucepan, combine orange juice, maple syrup, agave, guar gum, and grated orange rind, and cook for 5–10 minutes over medium heat.
2. Remove from heat and pour into a small bowl.
3. Chill for 2–3 hours before serving. Will keep for two weeks if refrigerated.

MAKES 1 CUP.

ORANGE TANGERINE MARMALADE

POWER 1

¹/₂ cup orange juice
¹/₃ cup tangerine juice
2 tablespoons pure maple syrup
2 tablespoons agave or other sweetener
2 teaspoons guar gum
1¹/₂ teaspoons orange rind, grated

1. In a medium-size saucepan, combine orange and tangerine juices, maple syrup, agave, guar gum, and grated orange rind, and cook for 5–10 minutes over medium heat.
2. Remove from heat and pour into a small bowl.
3. Chill for 2–3 hours before serving. Will keep for two weeks if refrigerated.

MAKES 1 CUP.

POLYNESIAN COCONUT NUT RICE

1 cup sweet rice, cooked
2 tablespoons unsweetened coconut, shredded
2 tablespoons cashews
2 tablespoons dried apricots, chopped
¹/₄ cup water
2 tablespoons sunflower seeds

1. Mix together rice, coconut, cashews, and apricots.
2. In a blender or food processor, purée half the mixture with the water, until coarsely ground.
3. Add puréed mixture back into the rest of the rice, and mix well.
4. Sprinkle with sunflower seeds.*
5. Serve immediately.

MAKES 1 SERVING.

Chef's Note: If desired, add rice, soy-, or almond milk to taste and for preferred consistency.

QUINOA CEREAL WITH PEARS AND SPICE

POWER 2

4 oranges (1 cup juice)
2 pears (¹/₂ cup pulp)
¹/₂ cup purified water
¹/₃ cup quinoa
¹/₃ cup whole dried papaya
3 tablespoons agave or other sweetener
¹/₂ teaspoon cinnamon
2 cups unsweetened rice milk, soymilk, or juice

1. Separately push the oranges and the pears through the juicer.
2. Set aside 1 cup of the orange juice and ½ cup of the pear pulp.
3. In a medium-size saucepan, combine the orange juice and water, and bring to a boil over high heat.
4. Reduce the heat to medium-low, and stir in the quinoa. Cook, uncovered, for 10–15 minutes, stirring occasionally.
5. Add the pear pulp, dried papaya, agave, and cinnamon, and cook for an additional 5–10 minutes, stirring occasionally.
6. Serve hot with unsweetened rice milk, soymilk, or juice.

MAKES 2 SERVINGS.

SOUTH PACIFIC RICE CEREAL

POWER 1

1/2 cup macadamia nuts, chopped
1 1/2 cups coconut milk
1 cup blueberries
1/2 cup papaya, chopped
1/2 cup pineapple, chopped
2 cups white basmati rice, cooked
1/4 cup unsweetened coconut, shredded
1 teaspoon coconut oil or macadamia nut oil

1. Preheat oven to 375°F.
2. Place nuts on an ungreased cookie sheet and bake for 10–15 minutes, or until light brown.
3. In a medium-size saucepan, combine the coconut milk, blueberries, papaya, and pineapple, and cook over medium-low heat for 3–5 minutes.
4. Add the cooked rice, coconut, coconut oil, and nuts. Mix well and cook an additional 2–3 minutes.*
5. Serve hot.

MAKES 2 SERVINGS.

Chef's Note: If desired, add rice, soy-, or almond milk to taste and for preferred consistency.

SWEET SPICE QUINOA

POWER 1

1 cup quinoa, cooked
½ cup peaches
1 tablespoon agave or other sweetener
dash nutmeg
dash allspice

1. In a small bowl, combine cooked quinoa, peaches, agave, nutmeg, and allspice.
2. Mix well.*
3. Serve immediately.

MAKES 1 SERVING.

*__Chef's Note:__ If desired, add rice, soy-, or almond milk to taste and for preferred consistency.

Chapter Five

APPETIZERS AND DIPS

BADASS BEAN DIP

POWER 3

1/2 cup cannellini beans (canned)
1/4 cup tahini
1/4 cup silken tofu
4 1/2 teaspoons fresh lemon juice
2 tablespoons fresh watercress, chopped
1 teaspoon soy sauce
1 teaspoon salt
1/4 teaspoon black pepper, freshly ground

1. In a blender or food processor, combine cannellini beans, tahini, tofu, lemon juice, watercress, soy sauce, salt, and pepper, and process until smooth.
2. Serve with pita bread, carrot sticks, or bread sticks.

MAKES ABOUT 1 1/4 CUPS.

FRESH HERBAL SPREAD

POWER 4

8 ounces soy cottage cheese
2 cloves garlic, finely chopped
3–4 scallions, finely chopped
¼ cup fresh parsley, finely chopped
¼ cup radishes, finely chopped
¼ cup fresh dill, finely chopped
¼ cup fresh basil, finely chopped
¼ cup black olives, finely chopped
1–2 tablespoons lemon juice
½ teaspoon mustard
½ teaspoon Worcestershire sauce

1. In a blender or food processor, combine soy cottage cheese, garlic, scallions, parsley, radishes, dill, basil, olives, lemon juice, mustard, and Worcestershire sauce, and blend well.
2. Refrigerate for at least 2 hours before serving to allow the flavors to blend.
3. Use for vegetable dip or spread on pita bread.

MAKES 1 CUP.

GOURMET SPICY TOFU DIP

POWER 2

2 cups silken tofu
2 tablespoons fresh basil, chopped
2 tablespoons fresh parsley, chopped
1/2 cup vegan mayonnaise
3 tablespoons prepared mustard
2 tablespoons apple cider vinegar
1 teaspoon balsamic vinegar
1/4 teaspoon lemon juice
1/4 teaspoon cayenne
3 teaspoons salt
3/4 teaspoon black pepper, freshly ground
paprika, as garnish

1. In a blender or food processor, combine tofu, basil, parsley, mayonnaise, mustard, cider vinegar, balsamic vinegar, lemon juice, cayenne, salt, and pepper, and blend until smooth.
2. Chill before serving.
3. Sprinkle with paprika, and serve with raw carrot and celery sticks, and broccoli and cauliflower florets.

MAKES 2½–3 CUPS.

HUMMUS TO MUMMUS

POWER 3

1 cup dried garbanzo beans
¹/₂ pound onions, minced
5 cloves garlic
¹/₄ cup fresh lemon juice
1 bunch dill, minced
¹/₄ cup sesame oil

1. Soak the garbanzo beans overnight in enough water to cover. Drain and cook the garbanzo beans in unsalted water for about 1 hour, or until they're soft enough to mash with a fork.
2. In a blender, combine the cooked garbanzo beans, liquid from the cooked garbanzo beans, onions, garlic, lemon juice, dill, and sesame oil, and blend until puréed.
3. Chill thoroughly.
4. Serve as a dip with crackers or pita bread, or use as a sandwich spread with sprouts and tomatoes.

MAKES 4½ CUPS.

NUTTY SOY CHEESE SPREAD

POWER 1

1½ cups soy cottage cheese
¾ cup currants
½ cup walnuts, chopped
⅓ cup figs, chopped
1 teaspoon cinnamon
1 teaspoon agave or other sweetener

1. Place soy cottage cheese in a mixing bowl. Beat briskly until it takes on a smooth texture.
2. Add currants, walnuts, figs, cinnamon, and agave, and mix thoroughly. A blender may also be used to combine the ingredients.
3. Use as a spread or as a filling on sandwiches. It tastes especially delicious on cinnamon raisin bread or date nut bread.

MAKES APPROXIMATELY 2–2½ CUPS.

SPICY EGGPLANT SPREAD

POWER 4

1 small eggplant
1 tablespoon onion, diced
1 tablespoon fresh tomato, chopped
1 tablespoon olive oil
1 teaspoon fresh lemon juice
¼ teaspoon garlic, crushed
1 tablespoon fresh parsley, chopped
¼ teaspoon cayenne
1 teaspoon salt
dash black pepper

1. Preheat oven to 375°F.
2. Broil eggplant in oven for 15–25 minutes, until it pops open.
   Remove the center with a spoon and discard the skin.
3. In a food processor or blender, run pulp through until mushy,
   and transfer to a mixing bowl.
4. Add the onion, tomato, oil, lemon juice, garlic, parsley,
   cayenne, salt, and pepper to the eggplant. Mix well.
5. Chill for 1–2 hours. Serve with crackers or pita bread.

MAKES ¼ CUP.

SPICY GINGER–BLACK BEAN PÂTÉ

POWER 7

1 cup black beans, cooked
1 tablespoon tamari
¼ teaspoon chili paste
1 tablespoon spelt flour
2 tablespoons toasted sesame oil, divided
2 cloves garlic, minced
1 teaspoon ginger, minced
2 tablespoons onion, chopped
2 tablespoons yellow pepper, chopped
¼ teaspoon sea salt
¼ cup soy cream cheese

1. Mash beans with a rice or potato masher.
2. Add tamari and chili paste, and stir to combine well.
3. Stir in flour and ½ tablespoon oil, and mix well.
4. In a pan, heat the remaining 1½ tablespoons toasted sesame oil, and sauté garlic, ginger, onion, yellow pepper, and salt.
5. Cook, stirring constantly, for 2 minutes.
6. Add garlic-ginger mixture to beans, stirring to combine thoroughly.
7. Whip cream cheese until fluffy.
8. Layer cream cheese and pâté in alternating ½-inch layers.
9. Refrigerate, but do not freeze. Serve with bread and crackers or with vegetables.

MAKES 2 SERVINGS.

SPICY RAW THAI ROLL-UPS

POWER 1

¹/₄ cup toasted coconut, shredded
¹/₄ cup cashews
¹/₂ lime or lemon, diced
1 teaspoon Thai chili paste
6 leaves young collard greens, trimmed

1. In a small bowl, mix together coconut, cashews, lime or lemon, and chili paste.
2. Drop spoonfuls of mixture on leaf of greens, and roll up.
3. Serve immediately.

MAKES 6 ROLLS.

SWEET ONION-CHEDDAR DELIGHT

POWER 2

¹/₂ cup soy cottage cheese
¹/₂ cup soy cheddar cheese, grated
1 tablespoon nondairy mayonnaise
1 small scallion, minced

1. In a blender, combine soy cottage cheese, grated cheese, mayonnaise, and scallion, and blend well.
2. This spread may be served with crackers immediately after preparation, but the flavor becomes even more delightful after the spread is chilled for 1 hour.

MAKES 1 CUP.

SWEET POTATO–BROCCOLI CREAM DIP

POWER 2

½ cup broccoli, chopped
1 cup sweet potato, peeled and cubed
1 cup silken tofu
½ cup tahini
4 tablespoons tamari
1 tablespoon scallions, chopped
¼ teaspoon black pepper, freshly ground

1. Steam broccoli 2–4 minutes.
2. Boil sweet potato until tender, about 20 minutes.
3. In a blender or food processor, combine broccoli, sweet potato, tofu, tahini, tamari, scallions, and black pepper, and process until smooth.
4. Serve cold with crackers or pita bread.

MAKES 2 CUPS.

TANGY TOMATO SALSA

POWER 3

1 cup fresh tomato, chopped
½ cup olives (of your choice), diced
¼ cup marinated sun-dried tomatoes, sliced
⅛–¼ cup onions, chopped
3–4 tablespoons fresh basil, chopped
3 tablespoons fresh parsley, chopped
2 tablespoons fresh hot peppers, minced (optional)
2 tablespoons olive oil (optional)
1 teaspoon flaxseed oil
2 teaspoons salt
½ teaspoon black pepper, freshly ground

1. In a medium-size bowl, combine tomato, olives, sun-dried tomatoes, onions, basil, parsley, hot peppers, olive oil, flaxseed oil, salt, and pepper, and stir until well mixed.
2. Chill 1–2 hours before serving with chips. It will keep in the refrigerator for two days, but stir before serving.

MAKES ABOUT 1½ CUPS.

TROPICAL SPICY GUACAMOLE

POWER 2

1 cup ripe avocado
2 tablespoons fresh lemon juice
2 tablespoons fresh lime juice
4 teaspoons sweet onion, diced
2 teaspoons fresh arugula, chopped
1 teaspoon salt
dash black pepper, freshly ground
1/2 teaspoon turmeric
1/8 teaspoon cayenne

1. In a medium-size bowl, combine avocado, lemon and lime juices, onion, arugula, salt, pepper, turmeric, and cayenne, and mash well with a fork.
2. Chill for 1 hour before serving with tortilla chips.

MAKES 1½ CUPS.

Chapter Six

SOUPS*

Chef's Note: If desired, add spring water to any of these recipes for your preferred consistency.

ANYTIME GAZPACHO

POWER 6

2 tomatoes, cored and quartered
1 red bell pepper, cored, seeded, and finely chopped
$^1/_2$ cucumber, peeled and cubed
$^1/_2$ teaspoon ginger, peeled and shredded
1 Vidalia onion, peeled and finely chopped
2 tablespoons parsley (flat-leafed preferred) or cilantro, finely chopped
2 cloves garlic, peeled and pressed
$^1/_8$ cup lemon juice, freshly squeezed (about 1 large lemon)
2 teaspoons lime juice
3 tablespoons olive oil
2 teaspoons sea salt
$^1/_4$ teaspoon black pepper, freshly ground
$^1/_4$ teaspoon cayenne
$^1/_3$ cup plain soy yogurt, as garnish (optional)
$^1/_3$ cup cherry tomatoes, halved, as garnish (optional)
$^1/_3$ cup fresh basil leaves, packed thinly sliced, as garnish (optional)

1. Push 1 tomato through the juicer. Set aside the juice. Dice the remaining tomato into ¼-inch cubes.
2. In a large bowl, combine the diced tomato, red pepper, cucumber, ginger, onion, parsley, and garlic.
3. Drizzle the tomato juice, lemon juice, lime juice, and olive oil onto the vegetables, and gently toss together until well coated.
4. Add salt, black pepper, and cayenne. Toss again.
5. In a blender or food processor, blend mixture until smooth.
6. Garnish with a dollop of soy yogurt, cherry tomatoes, and basil leaves, if desired.
7. Serve chilled.

MAKES 2 SERVINGS.

BASIC VEGETABLE STOCK

POWER 3

2 *summer squash* (¹/4 *cup juice, plus pulp*)
2 *stalks celery* (¹/4 *cup juice, plus pulp*)
4 *red peppers* (¹/4 *cup juice, plus pulp*)
3 *cups purified water*
1 *cup yellow onion, chopped*
2 *cloves garlic, crushed*
2 *tablespoons extra-virgin olive oil*
1 *teaspoon fresh basil, chopped, or* ¹/2 *teaspoon dried basil*
¹/2 *teaspoon mustard seeds*
2 *teaspoons sea salt*
¹/2 *teaspoon black pepper*
dash cayenne pepper or red pepper flakes
1 *teaspoon turmeric*

1. Separately push the squash, celery, and red peppers through
   the juicer. Set aside ¹/4 cup each of the squash, celery, and red
   pepper juice. Combine the squash, celery, and red pepper
   pulps, and set aside ¹/2 cup.
2. In a medium-size saucepan, combine the juices and pulp with
   the water, onion, garlic, olive oil, basil, mustard seeds, salt,
   pepper, cayenne pepper or red pepper flakes, and turmeric,
   and bring to a boil over high heat.
3. Reduce the heat to medium-low, and simmer, uncovered, for
   15 minutes.
4. Strain the soup stock through a fine colander or cheesecloth,
   collecting the liquid.
5. Serve hot as is, or use as a base for other soups.

MAKES 1 SERVING.

CARROT-POTATO SOUP

POWER 6

5 carrots, tops removed, halved lengthwise
1 piece gingerroot, cut into thirds (about 2-inch squares), peeled
1 lime, peeled
½ cup olive oil
1½ large Vidalia onions, peeled and finely chopped (about 2 cups)
5 cloves garlic, peeled and pressed
4 potatoes, peeled and diced, cooked
1 tablespoon plus 1 teaspoon grated ginger
1½ teaspoons sea salt
black pepper, freshly ground, to taste (optional)
2 cups purified water
1 large lime, sliced into quarters, as garnish (optional)
⅓ cup plain soy yogurt, as garnish (optional)
2 tablespoons parsley, finely chopped, as garnish (optional)

1. Push the carrots, ginger, and lime through the juicer.
2. Collect 1 cup of the pulp, and all of the juice, and set aside.
3. In a medium saucepan, heat oil and sauté the onions, garlic, potatoes, and ginger over moderate heat for 7–8 minutes.
4. When the onions become translucent, stir in the juice mixture, pulp, salt, pepper, if desired, and water. Simmer, partially covered, for 10 minutes.
5. Garnish with a lime wedge, a dollop of soy yogurt, and a sprinkling of parsley, if desired.
6. Serve hot or chilled.

MAKES 2 SERVINGS.

CHILLED ORANGE-CUCUMBER MINT SOUP

POWER 2

2 oranges, peeled (1 cup juice)
1 cucumber (¹/₂ cup juice)
4 stalks celery (1 cup juice)
2 cups spring water
3 tablespoons agave or rice syrup
1 cup plain soy yogurt
2 cucumbers, peeled and chopped
2 teaspoons fresh mint, finely chopped
4 tablespoons macadamia nut butter
2 teaspoons fresh parsley, chopped
¹/₄ cup red grapes, as garnish (optional)
2 fresh figs, sliced, as garnish (optional)

1. Juice the oranges, cucumber, and celery.
2. In a blender, combine the juices, spring water, agave, soy yogurt, cucumbers, mint, macadamia nut butter, and parsley, and blend well.
3. Chill for 1 hour.
4. Garnish with the red grapes and/or fresh figs, if desired.
5. Serve cold.

MAKES 2 SERVINGS.

CREAM OF BERRY SOUP

POWER 1

2 cups cherries, pitted, fresh or frozen
1 lemon, peeled and quartered
2 cups French vanilla soy creamer
1 cup raspberries or strawberries
1/4 cup tart dried cherries
1 tablespoon cranberry concentrate
1 tablespoon pomegranate concentrate
1/4 cup agar-agar
cinnamon, to taste, as garnish (optional)
1 kiwi, sliced into wedges, as garnish (optional)

1. Push the cherries and lemon through the juicer.
2. In a blender, combine the juice mixture, creamer, berries, dried cherries, cranberry and pomegranate concentrates, and agar-agar, and blend until smooth.
3. Garnish with cinnamon and kiwi slices, if desired.
4. Serve immediately.

MAKES 2 SERVINGS.

CREAM OF CAULIFLOWER-BROCCOLI SOUP

POWER 2

2 cups rice milk or soymilk
1 cup potatoes, cubed, steamed 15 minutes, until tender
1 cup broccoli florets, steamed 6 minutes
1/2 cup cauliflower florets, steamed 6 minutes
1 cup water
1 teaspoon salt
1/4 teaspoon black pepper, freshly ground
1/2 teaspoon fresh rosemary, chopped
1/4 cup onions, diced
1 1/2 teaspoons tamari

1. In a blender, combine rice milk or soymilk, potatoes, broccoli, cauliflower, water, salt, pepper, rosemary, onions, and tamari, and blend until smooth.
2. Pour into a medium-size saucepan and simmer over medium-low heat for 20 minutes.
3. Serve hot.

MAKES 2 SERVINGS.

CREAMY FENNEL-ACORN SOUP

POWER 2

1 acorn or Hubbard squash
¹/₂ tomato (¹/₄ cup juice)
2 cups soymilk
¹/₄ cup rice syrup
1 teaspoon fresh fennel
1 teaspoon fennel seed
¹/₄ teaspoon sea salt
¹/₄ teaspoon black pepper
1 cup chopped tomato (optional)
2 tablespoons plain soy yogurt, as garnish (optional)
2 sprigs fresh mint, as garnish (optional)
1 teaspoon soy Parmesan cheese, as garnish (optional)

1. Steam squash (with skin on) and purée.
2. Push tomato through the juicer.
3. In a medium-size saucepan, combine the squash purée, tomato juice, soymilk, rice syrup, fresh fennel, fennel seed, salt, and pepper. Bring to a simmer over medium-low heat and cook, uncovered, for 10–15 minutes.
4. Remove from heat.
5. Add chopped tomato, if desired.
6. Garnish with the yogurt, mint sprigs, and soy Parmesan cheese, if desired.
7. Serve hot or cold.

MAKES 2 SERVINGS.

CREAMY TOMATO-POTATO SOUP

POWER 4

2 cups potatoes, sliced
4 cups water
3 tablespoons toasted sesame oil
¹/₄ teaspoon cumin
¹/₄ teaspoon basil
1 cup French vanilla soy creamer
1 cup tomato, chopped
1 cup yellow pepper, chopped
¹/₂ cup scallions, chopped

1. Boil potatoes for approximately 15 minutes in 4 cups water.
2. Transfer potatoes and cooking water to blender. Add sesame oil, cumin, and basil, and purée until smooth.
3. Return mixture to saucepan and set on stove again over low heat.
4. Stir in the creamer, chopped tomato, pepper, and scallion, and cook for an additional 10–15 minutes.
5. Serve hot.

MAKES 2 SERVINGS.

CREAMY YUKON GOLD POTATO SOUP

POWER 2

2 tablespoons olive oil
³/4 cup Yukon Gold potatoes, peeled and cubed
¹/4 cup celery, sliced
¹/2 cup onions, diced
2 tablespoons parsnips, diced
1 teaspoon salt
2 cups water
1 vegetable bouillon cube (Morga)
1–2 cups rice milk or soymilk (depending on the consistency you like)
dash black pepper, freshly ground

1. In a large saucepan, heat the oil and sauté the potatoes, celery, onions, and parsnips over medium-high heat for 7–8 minutes.
2. Add the salt, water, bouillon, rice milk or soymilk, and pepper, and cook, covered, over medium-low heat for 25–30 minutes.
3. Serve hot.

MAKES 3 SERVINGS.

CURRIED CARROT SOUP

POWER 6

2 tablespoons coconut oil
1 onion, chopped
2 cloves garlic, chopped
2 teaspoons curry powder
2 tablespoons spelt or rice flour
3 carrots, tops removed, washed and chopped
4 cups vegetable stock
½ cup carrot juice (juice 1 or 2 carrots)
1½ cups soymilk
1 tablespoon agave or other sweetener
½ teaspoon cayenne pepper
salt, to taste
fresh ground pepper, to taste
2 tablespoons parsley or chives, chopped (optional)

1. In a large saucepan, heat the oil and sauté the onion and garlic with curry powder for 3–5 minutes. Stir in flour, carrots, and vegetable stock. Bring to a boil and simmer 25–30 minutes.
2. Juice carrots for ½ cup juice. Set aside.
3. Pour contents of saucepan into a blender or food processor, and blend well.
4. Return to saucepan and add carrot juice, soymilk, and agave.
5. Add cayenne, salt, and pepper, to taste.
6. Garnish with parsley or chives, if desired.
7. Serve hot.

MAKES 2 SERVINGS.

KICKING MISO SOUP

POWER 6

6 cups vegetable stock or water
1 onion, diced in ¼-inch pieces
3 cloves garlic, quartered or cut in large chunks
1 package firm tofu, diced in ½-inch cubes
1 teaspoon ginger, grated
1 cup shiitake mushrooms
½ cup mixed seaweed of choice: hijiki, kombu, kelp, nori
1 cup chard or collard greens, cut into bite-size chunks
2 tablespoons miso*
1 tablespoon parsley, lightly chopped
1 tablespoon wasabi
½ teaspoon cayenne
3 scallions, each sliced

1. Bring stock to a boil and turn down heat.
2. Simmer onion, garlic, tofu, ginger, mushrooms, seaweed, and chard or collard greens in vegetable stock for 5 minutes, then turn off heat.
3. In a small bowl, whisk together 2 tablespoons of miso with ½–1 cup broth, until fully dissolved. Add parsley, wasabi, cayenne, and scallions, and mix well.
4. Add miso mix back into original pot and stir well.
5. Serve immediately.

MAKES 6 SERVINGS.

Chef's Note: Never simmer miso; always add miso to a recipe after the cooking process is done. There are several types of miso available; experiment and use the one you like the best.

MEDITERRANEAN WHITE BEAN SOUP

POWER 3

¼ cup olive oil
¾ cup yellow or white onions, chopped
3 cups fresh tomatoes, chopped
½ cup white mushrooms, diced
½ cup small bow-tie whole grain pasta
¼ cup fresh parsley, chopped
1 cup white beans (canned)
3 teaspoons salt
½ teaspoon black pepper, freshly ground
2 cups water
pinch cayenne pepper

1. In a medium-size saucepan, heat oil and sauté the onions and tomatoes over medium-high heat for 5–7 minutes.
2. Add the remaining ingredients, reduce the heat to medium-low, cover, and cook for an additional 20–40 minutes.
3. Serve immediately.

MAKES 2–3 SERVINGS.

MISO TOFU VEGETABLE SOUP

POWER 7

4 carrots (³/4 cup juice), tops removed
4 cups purified water
1 pound firm tofu, cubed
1 bunch scallions, diced
1 cup whole shiitake mushrooms, destemmed
¹/4 cup snow pea pods
¹/4 cup cabbage, shredded
¹/2 teaspoon hot (spicy) sesame oil
1 tablespoon toasted sesame oil
1 teaspoon garlic, chopped
1 teaspoon fresh parsley, chopped
¹/2 teaspoon gingerroot, peeled and grated
¹/2 teaspoon red chili peppers, diced
¹/2 teaspoon turmeric
2 tablespoons brown rice miso

1. Push carrots through the juicer.
2. In a large saucepan, combine carrot juice, water, tofu, scallions, shiitake mushrooms, snow peas, cabbage, hot and toasted sesame oils, garlic, parsley, ginger, chili peppers, and turmeric, and bring to a boil over high heat.
3. Reduce the heat to medium-low and simmer, uncovered, for 15–20 minutes.
4. Remove from heat, dissolve the miso in the mixture, and stir well.*
5. Serve hot with whole grain bread.

MAKES 2 SERVINGS.

Chef's Note: Never simmer miso; always add miso to a recipe after the cooking process is done. There are several types of miso available; experiment and use the one you like the best.

MMMM . . . MELON MACADAMIA SOUP

POWER 2

2 cups cantaloupe, rind removed, diced (juiced, reserve pulp)
1 cup honeydew, peeled and diced (juiced, reserve pulp)
2 pears (1 cup juiced)
1½ cups unsweetened soymilk
1 teaspoon vanilla extract
¾ teaspoon cinnamon
pinch sea salt
¼ teaspoon cardamom
2 ripe bananas, peeled
1 cup macadamia nuts, raw and unsalted
fresh figs, sliced, as garnish (optional)

1. Separately juice melons. Reserve the pulp.
2. Juice the pears.
3. In a medium-size saucepan, combine pulp, juice, soymilk, vanilla extract, cinnamon, salt, and cardamom. Bring to a gentle simmer.
4. In a blender, combine bananas and nuts. Blend on low.
5. Gently drizzle ¼–½ cup of soup through the top of the mixing blender until creamy.
6. Stir banana nut cream back into remaining soup.
7. Garnish with sliced fresh figs, if desired.
8. Serve chilled or warm.

MAKES 2 SERVINGS.

MUSHROOM TOFU RICE SOUP

POWER 3

2 tablespoons olive oil
1 cup leeks or scallions, sliced
5½ cups purified water
1 yellow onion, diced
2 cups shiitake or baby portobello mushrooms, sliced
1 cup zucchini, chopped
1 cup firm tofu, cubed
½ cup basmati–wild rice mix
2 teaspoons sea salt
1 teaspoon black pepper
dash cayenne
¼ cup sprouts (optional)

1. In a large saucepan, heat the oil and sauté the leeks or scallions until soft.
2. Add the water, onion, mushrooms, zucchini, tofu, rice, salt, pepper, and cayenne, and bring to a boil over high heat.
3. Reduce the heat to medium-low, and simmer, covered, for 30–35 minutes, or until done.
4. Garnish with sprouts, if desired.
5. Serve hot.

MAKES 2 SERVINGS.

OLD-TIME MUSHROOM BARLEY SOUP

POWER 3

3 tablespoons olive oil
2 cups white button mushrooms, sliced
¹/₂ cup shiitake mushrooms, sliced
1 cup leeks, sliced
¹/₂ cup broccoli, diced
¹/₂ cup onions, diced
³/₄ cup barley, cooked
2¹/₂ cups water
3 tablespoons fresh tarragon, chopped
3 teaspoons sea salt
¹/₂ teaspoon black pepper, freshly ground
pinch cayenne pepper

1. In a large saucepan, heat oil and sauté the mushrooms, leeks, broccoli, and onions for 3–5 minutes over medium-high heat.
2. Add barley, water, tarragon, salt, pepper, and cayenne, and cook, covered, over medium-low heat for 35–45 minutes.
3. Serve immediately.

MAKES 3 SERVINGS.

ONION SHIITAKE SOUP

POWER 3

1/4 cup olive oil
4 cups yellow onions, sliced
2 cups shiitake mushrooms, sliced
1/4 cup fresh parsley, chopped
4 cups water
2 vegetable bouillon cubes (Morga)
1/2 teaspoon black pepper, freshly ground
2 1/4 teaspoons basil, dried
1 1/2 teaspoons garlic powder
2 tablespoons sweet miso paste

1. In a large saucepan, heat the oil and sauté the onions, shiitake mushrooms, and parsley over medium-high heat, until the onions are translucent.
2. Add the water, bouillon, pepper, basil, and garlic powder. Stir well.
3. Reduce the heat to medium and cook, covered, for 20 minutes.
4. Remove from heat and whisk in miso paste, stirring until dissolved.*
5. Serve immediately.

MAKES 2–3 SERVINGS.

Chef's Note: Never simmer miso; always add miso to a recipe after the cooking process is done. There are several types of miso available; experiment and use the one you like the best.

ORIENTAL MUSHROOM SOUP

POWER 5

1 tablespoon toasted sesame oil
1/4 teaspoon hot sesame oil
1/2 cup leeks, chopped
3 scallions, chopped
3 tablespoons tamari
2 cloves garlic, sliced
2 teaspoons ginger, freshly grated
1/2 cup firm tofu, diced
5 cups water
1/2 cup water chestnuts (measured, then chopped)
1/2 cup bamboo shoots (measured, then chopped)

1/4 cup dried black mushrooms
1/4 cup tree ear mushrooms
1/2 cup shiitake mushrooms, heads only, sliced
1/2 teaspoon black pepper, freshly ground
1/2 cup kombu sea vegetable, chopped
pinch cayenne pepper
1/2 cup mild-sweet miso paste
1 tablespoon nori flakes, as garnish (optional)

1. In a large saucepan, heat the oils and sauté the leeks and scallions over medium-high heat for 5 minutes.
2. Add the tamari, garlic, ginger, and tofu, and sauté another 3 minutes.
3. Add water, water chestnuts, bamboo shoots, mushrooms, black pepper, sea vegetables, and cayenne. Reduce the heat to low and let simmer, uncovered, for 50 minutes.
4. Remove from heat and whisk in miso paste, stirring until dissolved.*
5. Garnish with the nori flakes, if desired.
6. Serve immediately.

MAKES 3 SERVINGS.

*Chef's Note: Never simmer miso; always add miso to a recipe after the cooking process is done. There are several types of miso available; experiment and use the one you like the best.

ORIENTAL NOODLE SOUP

POWER 4

1/4 cup olive oil
1/2 cup zucchini, sliced
1/2 cup cauliflower florets
1/2 cup carrots, sliced
1/2 cup sea vegetables (wakame-hijiki)
1/2 cup potatoes, sliced
1/2 cup celery, sliced
1/4 cup onions, diced
1/4 cup shiitake mushrooms, sliced
7 cups water
1/4 cup fresh parsley, chopped
1 teaspoon salt
1/4 teaspoon black pepper, freshly ground
1 vegetable bouillon cube (Morga)
2 bay leaves
1/4 cup fresh dill, chopped
2 cups rice noodles, uncooked
2 tablespoons rice or barley miso paste

1. In a large saucepan, heat the oil and sauté the zucchini, cauliflower, carrots, sea vegetables, potatoes, celery, onions, and shiitake mushrooms over medium heat for about 10 minutes.
2. Add water, parsley, salt, pepper, bouillon, bay leaves, and dill, and let simmer over medium-low heat 15–25 minutes.
3. Add the noodles and simmer for 10 minutes more.
4. Remove from heat and whisk in miso paste, stirring until dissolved.*
5. Serve immediately.

MAKES 4 SERVINGS.

Chef's Note: Never simmer miso; always add miso to a recipe after the cooking process is done. There are several types of miso available; experiment and use the one you like the best.

PAPAYA YAM SOUP

2–3 yams (1¹/₄ cups juice, ¹/₂ cup pulp)
2 papayas (1 cup juice)
2¹/₂–3 cups purified water
¹/₂ teaspoon nutmeg, ground
¹/₈ teaspoon cinnamon
¹/₂ teaspoon cardamom
*5 tablespoons arrowroot or equivalent kudzu (prepared per package
    instructions)*
¹/₄ cup papaya, sliced, as garnish (optional)
¹/₄ cup fresh cherries or red grapes, as garnish (optional)

1. Separately push the yams and papayas through the juicer. Set
   aside 1¼ cups of the yam juice, ½ cup of the yam pulp, and 1
   cup of the papaya juice.
2. In a medium-size saucepan, combine the juices, pulp, water,
   nutmeg, cinnamon, and cardamom, and bring to a boil over
   high heat.
3. Reduce the heat to medium-low.
4. Gradually stir in arrowroot mixture, and simmer, uncovered,
   for 7–10 minutes, or until arrowroot thickens.
5. Garnish with the papaya slices and red grapes, if desired.
6. Serve hot or cold.

MAKES 2 SERVINGS.

PARSNIP–BLACK BEAN SOUP

POWER 2

1½ *cups black beans, canned, or* ⅓ *cup dried beans**
½ *cup parsnips, chopped into* ½-*inch cubes*
4 *cups purified water*
1 *cup corn (fresh or off the cob)*
1 *cup tofu, cut into* ½-*inch cubes*
3 *tablespoons fresh chives, minced*
3 *tablespoons coconut oil*
1 *teaspoon salt*
½ *teaspoon cumin*

1. In a large saucepan, heat canned beans in 6 ounces of water and bring to a boil.
2. In a separate saucepan, boil parsnips until tender.
3. Lower heat to medium on the saucepan with the beans and add water, parsnips, corn, tofu, chives, coconut oil, salt, and cumin. Mix well.
4. In a blender, purée half of this mixture for 15 seconds.
5. Add puréed mixture back to the rest of the soup.
6. Cook for additional 30 minutes over low heat.
7. Serve hot.

MAKES 3 SERVINGS.

Chef's Note: If using dried beans, soak overnight in 32 ounces of water. In the morning, rinse well and add 40 ounces of fresh water. Bring beans and fresh water to a boil, lower heat to medium, and cover. Cook for about one hour, and then follow steps 2–6.

PARSNIP-POTATO SOUP

POWER 2

1 potato, steamed and chilled (¹/₂ cup juice, ¹/₂ tablespoon pulp)
2 stalks celery (¹/₂ cup juice)
1 tablespoon olive oil
¹/₄ cup leeks, chopped
1 parsnip, peeled, boiled
¹/₂ cup potatoes, cubed
3 cups unsweetened soymilk
¹/₂ teaspoon fresh basil, finely chopped
1 teaspoon fresh fennel, finely chopped
¹/₄ teaspoon mustard seed
1 teaspoon sea salt
¹/₄–¹/₂ teaspoon black pepper
1 teaspoon soy sauce
4 sprigs fresh mint, as garnish (optional)

1. Juice the potato and celery separately. Set aside ½ cup of the potato juice, ½ tablespoon of the potato pulp, and ½ cup of the celery juice.
2. In a large saucepan, heat the oil and sauté the leeks and parsnip for 3–4 minutes.
3. Combine with the juices, pulp, potatoes, soymilk, basil, fennel, mustard seed, salt, pepper, and soy sauce, and bring to a boil over high heat.
4. Reduce the heat to medium-low, and simmer, uncovered, for 10 minutes, or until the potatoes are tender
5. Garnish with mint sprigs, if desired.
6. Serve hot.

MAKES 2 SERVINGS.

PASTA CANNELLINI SOUP

POWER 7

3 cucumbers (1½ cups juice)
½ head broccoli, steamed and
   chilled (½ cup pulp)
3 tablespoons olive oil
½ cup yellow onion, diced
2 cups purified water
1½ cups tomatoes, chopped
¾ cups cannellini beans, cooked
½ cup escarole or kale, chopped
¼ cup celery, chopped

¼ cup carrots, sliced
¼ cup whole grain macaroni,
   uncooked
2 teaspoons fresh parsley, chopped
2 teaspoons fresh basil, chopped
1 teaspoon sea salt
½ teaspoon black pepper
1 clove garlic, crushed
dash cayenne pepper
2 teaspoons sweet miso

1. Separately push the cucumbers and broccoli through the juicer. Set aside 1½ cups of the cucumber juice and ½ cup of the broccoli pulp.
2. In a large saucepan, heat the oil and sauté the onion for 2–3 minutes.
3. Add the cucumber juice, broccoli pulp, and water to the saucepan, and bring to a boil over high heat.
4. Reduce the heat to medium-low, add tomatoes, beans, escarole or kale, celery, carrots, macaroni, parsley, basil, salt, pepper, garlic, and cayenne, and simmer, uncovered, for 15 minutes, or until the pasta is tender.
5. Remove from heat and whisk in the miso, stirring until dissolved.*
6. Serve hot or cold with bread.

MAKES 2–4 SERVINGS.

*Chef's Note: Never simmer miso; always add miso to a recipe after the cooking process is done. There are several types of miso available; experiment and use the one you like the best.

SANTA FE SQUASH SOUP

POWER 4

2 pounds acorn squash (or any other squash), peeled (approximately one squash)
1 cup black beans, cooked
¼ cup purified water
2 tablespoons plain soy yogurt
2 cups tomato, chopped
1 teaspoon fresh basil, chopped, or ½ teaspoon dried basil
1 yellow pepper, minced
½ teaspoon jalapeño pepper, finely chopped
½ teaspoon fresh rosemary, finely chopped
¼ teaspoon cayenne
2 tablespoons tomato, chopped, as garnish (optional)
2 sprigs fresh mint, as garnish (optional)
1 tablespoon pine nuts, as garnish (optional)

1. Push the squash through the juicer. Set aside 1 cup of the juice.
2. In a blender or food processor, combine the black beans with the water, and blend until smooth.
3. In a medium-size saucepan, combine squash juice, black bean purée, and soy yogurt, and whisk until creamy.
4. Add the tomato, basil, yellow pepper, jalapeño pepper, rosemary, and cayenne. Simmer, uncovered, over medium-low heat for 5–10 minutes.
5. Garnish with tomato, mint, and pine nuts, if desired.
6. Serve hot or cold.

MAKES 2 SERVINGS.

SPICY GINGERY LIMA BEAN SOUP

POWER 3

2 acorn squash, peeled and cored before juicing (1 cup juice,
   ¹/₂ cup pulp)
3 tomatoes, chopped
2³/₄–3 cups purified water
¹/₃ cup lima beans, cooked
¹/₈ cup tamari
1 tablespoon fresh parsley, chopped
4 teaspoons ginger powder
¹/₄ teaspoon sea salt
¹/₈ teaspoon turmeric
¹/₈ teaspoon wasabi powder
¹/₈ teaspoon black pepper

1. Push the squash through the juicer. Set aside 1 cup of the squash juice and ¹/₂ cup of the squash pulp.
2. In a medium-size saucepan, combine the juice and pulp with the tomatoes, water, lima beans, tamari, parsley, ginger powder, salt, turmeric, wasabi powder, and black pepper, and bring to a boil over high heat.
3. Reduce the heat to medium-low and simmer, uncovered, for 10–12 minutes.
4. Serve hot with whole grain bread.

MAKES 2 SERVINGS.

SPICY RAW SPINACH AND AVOCADO SOUP

POWER 4

1 cucumber (1/2 cup cucumber juice)
2 cups spinach, washed and chopped
2 cups tomatoes, cubed
1/2 ripe avocado
1/2-inch slice ginger
1/4 cup flaxseed oil
1 clove garlic, minced
1 tablespoon lemon
1 tablespoon apple cider vinegar
1/2 teaspoon light miso
1/2 teaspoon salt
1/2 teaspoon cayenne
1 teaspoon chia, as garnish (optional)
1 teaspoon flaxseeds, as garnish (optional)

1. Push cucumber through juicer and set aside 1/2 cup juice.
2. In a blender, combine cucumber juice, spinach, tomatoes, avocado, ginger, flaxseed oil, garlic, lemon, cider vinegar, miso, salt, and cayenne, and blend until smooth.
3. Chill for 1–2 hours.
4. Garnish with chia or flaxseeds, if desired.
5. Serve chilled.

MAKES 4 SERVINGS.

SWEET AND SOUR SOUP

POWER 4

5 cups Basic Vegetable Stock (see recipe, page 154)
1 cup apple juice
1 cup lentils
1 carrot, sliced
1 stalk celery, sliced
1 teaspoon garlic powder
1 teaspoon onion powder
2 teaspoons parsley flakes
2 tablespoons apple cider vinegar
1 tablespoon tamari

1. In a medium-size soup pot, combine the stock and the apple juice and bring to a boil.
2. Add lentils, carrot, celery, garlic powder, onion powder, and parsley, and bring the mixture back to a boil.
3. Lower the heat to medium-low and simmer for 30 minutes.
4. Add vinegar and tamari. Continue to simmer for about 20 minutes more, or until the lentils are soft.
5. Serve immediately.

MAKES 4 SERVINGS.

TART CHERRY AND RASPBERRY SOUP

POWER 1

1 cup cherry juice
1 cup unsweetened cherries, pitted
¼ cup dried tart raspberries
1 cup unsweetened soymilk
3 tablespoons agave or other sweetener
1 cinnamon stick

1. In a blender, combine cherry juice, cherries, raspberries, soymilk, and agave, and blend until smooth.
2. Pour the mixture into a medium-size saucepan, add the cinnamon stick, and bring to a simmer over medium-low heat.
3. Cook 2–3 minutes, until thickened.
4. Remove from heat and remove cinnamon stick.
5. Chill 1–2 hours.
6. Serve cold.

MAKES 2 SERVINGS.

TRINIDADIAN SQUASH SOUP

2 cups butternut squash
2 cups purified water
2 tablespoons sunflower seeds, raw
2 teaspoons maple syrup
1 teaspoon curry
pinch cinnamon
½ cup celery, chopped

1. Preheat oven to 400°F.
2. Cut squash in half. Remove the seeds and discard them. Place squash in a baking pan, cut side down, with ⅓ inch water. Bake for 40 minutes.
3. When cooled, remove the skin and place the squash in a blender with water, sunflower seeds, maple syrup, curry, and cinnamon, and blend until smooth.
4. Transfer squash mixture to medium-size saucepan, add chopped celery, and mix well.
5. Cook over low heat for about 20 minutes, or until thoroughly heated.
6. Serve immediately.

MAKES 2 SERVINGS.

Chapter Seven

SALADS

AFRICAN MILLET SALAD

POWER 4

1 cup adzuki beans, cooked and chilled
1 teaspoon mint
1 cup millet, cooked and chilled
1 cup red pepper, chopped
1/2 cup sweet onion, chopped
pinch celery seed
1 teaspoon salt
1/2 teaspoon tarragon
2 tablespoons toasted sesame oil

1. In a large bowl, combine beans, mint, millet, red pepper, onion, celery seed, salt, and tarragon, and mix well.
2. Drizzle sesame oil over salad.
3. Serve cold.

MAKES 2 SERVINGS.

ARAME FENNEL SALAD

1 cup arame
½ cup fennel
½ cup daikon radish, shredded
¼ cup toasted sesame oil
4–6 tablespoons rice vinegar or apple cider vinegar
2 tablespoons lemon juice
1 teaspoon salt
¼ teaspoon black pepper, freshly ground
2 tablespoons sesame seeds

1. Soak arame in hot water, covered, for 15 minutes.
2. Drain, rinse, cover with fresh water, and then boil for 15 minutes.
3. Drain and measure 1 cup.
4. In a large bowl, combine arame, fennel, and daikon radish, and mix well.
5. In a small bowl, whisk together sesame oil, vinegar, lemon juice, salt, and pepper.
6. Pour over arame mixture and toss well.
7. Chill for 1 hour before serving. Garnish with sesame seeds.

MAKES 2 SERVINGS.

ARTICHOKE–GARBANZO BEAN SALAD

POWER 5

1 cup garbanzo beans, cooked
1 cup couscous, cooked
½ cup marinated artichoke hearts (jarred)
½ cup fresh parsley, chopped
½ cup fresh dill, chopped
2 tablespoons fresh mint, chopped
1½ teaspoons garlic, crushed
2 tablespoons scallions, sliced
½ cup fresh tomatoes, chopped (optional)
¼ cup olive oil
1 tablespoon fresh lemon juice
1½ teaspoons salt

1. In a large bowl, combine beans, couscous, artichoke hearts, parsley, dill, mint, garlic, scallions, and tomatoes, if desired.
2. In a small bowl, whisk together olive oil, lemon juice, and salt.
3. Pour dressing over salad and toss well.
4. Serve immediately.

MAKES 4 SERVINGS.

Broccoli Wild Rice

Tempeh Marinara with Rice Penne

Mediterranean Bean Salad

Endive with Basil and Sprouts

Acorn Squash Bake

Mango Cabbage Salad

Healthy Hijiki

New Southern Greens

Very Berry Smoothie

Spicy Raw Spinach and Avocado Soup

Anytime Gazpacho

Cream of Berry Soup

Hawaiian Coconut Buckwheat Cereal

Our fine artist, Melissa Goldman

Preparing the recipes at Gary's home kitchen: (left to right) Bryan Hantman, Doreen Starling, Claire Adams, Lydia Semczyszyn, Christina Stevens

The juicebar guys at Gary Null's Uptown Wholefoods: (left to right) Nazmul Khandaker and Asiruddin Ahmed

Chefs for Gary Null's Uptown Wholefoods: (left to right) Mohammad Hossain, Mizael Vasquez, Felipe Montealegre, Shelly Null, Guadelpe Cortez, Edgar Duran, and Serafin Gonzalez

ASPARAGUS SALAD

POWER 1

24 green asparagus
16 white asparagus
¼ cup olive oil
¼ cup water
2 tablespoons lemon juice, or to taste
pinch sea salt
pinch black pepper
4 thin slices pickled ginger
dash wasabi, as garnish (optional)

1. Place the asparagus in medium-size pan and blanch, approximately 2–3 minutes.
2. In a small bowl, whisk together olive oil, water, lemon juice, salt, pepper, and pickled ginger.
3. Arrange asparagus on a platter and drizzle with dressing.
4. Garnish with wasabi, if desired.
5. Serve immediately.

MAKES 6–8 SERVINGS.

BANGKOK SALAD

POWER 4

1 cup bean threads
1 cup sweet onion, grated
¼ cup cucumber, thinly sliced
4 ounces firm tofu, sliced into thin 2-inch strips
1 stalk lemongrass, thinly sliced
⅛ cup fresh lime juice
1 teaspoon rice vinegar
2 red chile peppers, seeded and chopped
10 mint leaves
2 scallions, tops included, chopped
1 cup chickpeas, cooked
1 tablespoon fresh parsley, chopped
3 teaspoons agave or other sweetener
1 tablespoon fresh mustard
⅛ teaspoon allspice
1 small Boston lettuce
radish slices, as garnish (optional)

1. Cover bean threads in warm water and soak for 15 minutes.
2. Drain and slice into 3-inch strips.
3. In a bowl, combine bean threads, onion, cucumber, tofu, lemongrass, lime juice, rice vinegar, red peppers, mint leaves, scallions, chickpeas, parsley, agave, mustard, and allspice.
4. Line a salad bowl with Boston lettuce leaves, and spoon salad mixture into center.
5. Garnish with radish slices, if desired.
6. Serve immediately.

MAKES 2 SERVINGS.

BASIC VINAIGRETTE

¼ cup balsamic vinegar or lemon juice
¾–1 cup olive oil, to taste
1 tablespoon Dijon mustard
salt and pepper, to taste

1. Whisk ingredients together.
2. Drizzle dressing over salad before tossing.
3. Serve immediately.

CHINA SEA SEAWEED SALAD

POWER 3

½ cup hijiki (1 ounce dry)
2 tablespoons olive oil
3 ounces carrots, cut in long, thin strips
½ cup daikon, cut in long, thin strips
½ cup scallions, chopped
1 teaspoon garlic, minced
½ teaspoon caraway seeds
½ teaspoon salt
1 cup millet, cooked and chilled

1. Rinse hijiki three times, cover with water and soak for 10 minutes, drain, and place in bowl.
2. In a skillet, heat oil and lightly sauté carrots, daikon, and scallions for about 5 minutes.
3. Combine hijiki, sautéed mix, garlic, caraway seeds, salt, and millet. Mix well.
4. Serve immediately.

MAKES 2 SERVINGS.

CHRISTINA'S VINAIGRETTE

POWER 1

½ cup apple cider vinegar
1 teaspoon lemon juice
2 tablespoons Dijon mustard
1 tablespoon tahini
1 tablespoon agave or other sweetener
2 cloves garlic, peeled
1¼ cups extra-virgin olive oil
½ cup flaxseed oil
1 tablespoon parsley, lightly chopped
1 teaspoon thyme, lightly chopped
1 teaspoon rosemary, lightly chopped
1 teaspoon tarragon (fresh)
white ground pepper, to taste

1. In a blender, combine vinegar, lemon juice, mustard, tahini, agave, and garlic.
2. While blending, slowly drizzle the oils into the mix until the vinaigrette becomes creamy.
3. After all the oil has been incorporated, add the parsley, thyme, rosemary, and tarragon, and mix well. Season with white pepper to taste.
4. Drizzle over salad before tossing.
5. Serve immediately.

COLESLAW WITH FRESH FENNEL

POWER 1

2 lemons (3 tablespoons juice)
2 limes (2 tablespoons juice)
2 cups green cabbage, shredded
1/2 cup fennel
3 tablespoons soy mayonnaise
1 tablespoon pickled relish
1 teaspoon prepared mustard
1 tablespoon fresh dill, chopped
1 teaspoon sea salt
1/4 teaspoon black pepper
dash apple cider vinegar
dash cayenne

1. Juice the lemons and limes.
2. In a medium-size mixing bowl, toss the juice with the cabbage, fennel, mayonnaise, relish, mustard, dill, salt, pepper, vinegar, and cayenne.
3. Serve cold as a salad or a sandwich filling.

MAKES 2 SERVINGS.

CUCUMBER-ARAME SALAD

POWER 3

4 cups arame
1 cup carrot, cut into tiny cubes
1 cup cucumber, sliced
1/2 cup yellow pepper, sliced
1/4 cup sesame seeds
1/4 cup apple cider vinegar
3 tablespoons olive oil
3 tablespoons mustard
2 tablespoons agave or other sweetener
1 tablespoon lemon juice
dash cayenne

1. Cover arame in hot water and soak for 15 minutes.
2. Drain, rinse, cover with fresh water, and then boil for 15 minutes.
3. Drain and measure 4 cups.
4. Steam carrot cubes lightly.
5. In a large bowl, combine arame, carrot, cucumber, pepper, and sesame seeds.
6. In a small bowl, whisk vinegar, olive oil, mustard, agave, lemon juice, and cayenne.
7. Drizzle over salad and toss well.
8. Serve immediately.

MAKES 4 SERVINGS.

ENDIVE WITH BASIL AND SPROUTS

POWER 3

1 cup curly or Belgian endive, torn
1 cup Mesclun lettuce, torn
1/2 cup basil leaves, firmly packed
1/2 cup clover sprouts
1 cup fresh tomatoes, chopped
1 cup blueberries, as garnish (optional)
1/2 cup pears, diced, as garnish (optional)
1/2 cup toasted pumpkin seeds, as garnish (optional)

1. In a large salad bowl, combine the endive, lettuce, basil, sprouts, and tomatoes.
2. Garnish with blueberries, pears, and pumpkin seeds, if desired.
3. Serve with a favorite salad dressing.

MAKES 2 SERVINGS.

GARDEN BUCKWHEAT SALAD

POWER 3

3 cups buckwheat noodles, cooked
1 cup broccoli florets, steamed 5–6 minutes
1 cup carrots, sliced
¼ cup gomasio
2 tablespoons scallions, sliced
2 tablespoons raisins
2 tablespoons sunflower seeds
¼ cup toasted sesame oil
3–4 tablespoons tamari

1. In a medium-size bowl, combine noodles, broccoli, carrots, gomasio, scallions, raisins, and sunflower seeds.
2. Add sesame oil and tamari and mix well.
3. Serve chilled.

MAKES 2 SERVINGS.

HAVE-A-LOTTA INSALATA

POWER 4

1/2 cup cauliflower florets
1/2 cup broccoli florets
1/2 cup arugula, chopped
1/2 cup cherry tomatoes, chopped
1/2 red pepper, diced
1/2 yellow pepper, diced
1/4 cup artichoke hearts, chopped
1/2 pound baby bella mushrooms, sliced
12 green and black olives, pitted, deli style
1/2 cup peas
1/2 teaspoon fresh basil
1 1/2 tablespoons capers
1 cup cannellini beans (canned)
sea salt, to taste
black pepper, freshly ground, to taste
1/2 teaspoon lemon juice
1/4 cup extra-virgin olive oil
1/8 cup balsamic vinegar

1. In a salad bowl, toss together cauliflower, broccoli, arugula, tomatoes, red and yellow pepper, artichoke hearts, mushrooms, olives, peas, basil, capers, and beans.
2. Season with salt and pepper.
3. In a small bowl, whisk together lemon juice, oil, and balsamic vinegar.
4. Pour dressing over salad and toss lightly.
5. Serve immediately.

MAKES 2 SERVINGS.

INDIAN ARUGULA SALAD

POWER 3

3 cups cucumbers, peeled and chopped
2 cups plain soy yogurt
1½ cups tomatoes, chopped
1 cup fresh arugula, torn
1 tablespoon lemon juice
1 tablespoon flaxseed oil
2 teaspoons cardamom, ground
1 teaspoon apple cider vinegar
1 teaspoon sea salt
1 teaspoon toasted sesame seeds
⅛ teaspoon turmeric
dash cayenne pepper

1. In a large bowl, combine cucumbers, soy yogurt, tomatoes, and arugula, and mix well.
2. In a small bowl, whisk together lemon juice, flaxseed oil, cardamom, vinegar, sea salt, sesame seeds, turmeric, and cayenne.
3. Toss the salad with the desired amount of dressing.
4. Serve at room temperature.

MAKES 2 SERVINGS.

LIMA BEAN–SEAWEED SALAD

POWER 1

1 cup wakame (1 ounce dry)
12 ice cubes
1 cup snap beans, cut into 1-inch pieces
1 teaspoon dill
3–4 tablespoons tamari
1 teaspoon tarragon
1 cup garbanzo beans, cooked
1 cup lima beans, cooked
1 teaspoon salt
1 teaspoon lemon
2 tablespoons olive oil

1. Rinse and soak wakame for 10 minutes in water to cover, then cook at a low temperature for 20 minutes still covered in water.
2. Submerge wakame in a bowl of ice water to avoid overcooking.
3. Chill wakame in refrigerator.
4. Steam snap beans for 10 minutes.
5. In a bowl, combine wakame, snap beans, dill, tamari, tarragon, garbanzo beans, lima beans, salt, lemon, and olive oil, and toss well.
6. Serve chilled.

MAKES 2 SERVINGS.

LIVING-IT-UP POTATO SALAD

6 potatoes (a variety for color, taste, and texture: sweet, blue, russet,
  red, and yellow)
⅓ cup crunchy sprouts
⅓ cup fresh parsley, chopped
½ cup olive oil
⅙ cup balsamic vinegar
⅛ cup tamari or wheat-free soy sauce
2 teaspoons cayenne
1 teaspoon cumin
salt and pepper, to taste

1. Bake potatoes at 400°F for 30–40 minutes, or until soft
   (insert fork to see how easily it goes through potatoes). Allow
   potatoes to cool completely.
2. Cut potatoes into large chunks, approximately 6–8 chunks per
   potato. Place potatoes in a large bowl. Add sprouts and
   parsley.
3. In a separate bowl, whisk together olive oil, vinegar, tamari or
   soy sauce, cayenne, cumin, salt, and pepper.
4. Drizzle dressing over potato salad and mix well.
5. Serve cooled.

MAKES 4 SERVINGS.

MAJOR SPROUT SALAD

POWER 2

2½ *cups mixed crunchy sprouts*
1½ *cups sunflower sprouts*
1 *cup yellow pepper, sliced*
½ *cup heart of palm, quartered*
½ *cup artichoke hearts*
2 *beets, quartered*
½ *sweet onion, sliced*
salad dressing to taste

1. In a large mixing bowl, toss sprouts, pepper, heart of palm, artichoke hearts, beets, and onion with desired amount of favorite dressing.
2. Serve at room temperature.

MAKES 2 SERVINGS.

MANGO CABBAGE SALAD

POWER 1

4 cups red cabbage, shredded
¼ cup mango, diced
¼ cup olive oil
2 tablespoons lemon juice
4 tablespoons lime juice
2 tablespoons agave or other sweetener
4 tablespoons fresh basil, minced
2 tablespoons mint, minced
fanned mango segments and edible flowers (if available), as garnish
   (optional)

1. In a large bowl, toss together cabbage and mango.
2. In a separate bowl, whisk together oil, lemon juice, lime juice, agave, basil, and mint.
3. Pour dressing over salad, and toss well.
4. Marinate in refrigerator for 1 hour before serving.
5. Garnish the plate with a flower and fanned mango segments, if desired.
6. Serve chilled.

MAKES 2 SERVINGS.

MEDITERRANEAN BEAN SALAD

P O W E R   3

2 cups cannellini beans, cooked
2 cloves garlic, peeled and minced
1 tablespoon lemon juice
1 tablespoon thyme
1 tablespoon rosemary
2 scallions, chopped
1 container crunchy sprouts
2 cups field greens
½ cup vinaigrette (see recipe, pages 187 or 188)

1. In a large bowl, combine beans, garlic, lemon juice, thyme, rosemary, scallions, and crunchy sprouts.
2. Serve on a bed of field greens, dressed with vinaigrette.

MAKES 4 SERVINGS.

MIXED MUSHROOMS SALAD
WITH HEARTS OF PALM

POWER 3

2 tablespoons olive oil
1 cup shiitake mushrooms, stemmed and quartered
1 cup white mushrooms, stemmed and sliced
1 cup portobello mushrooms, stemmed and sliced, with gills removed
1/2 onion, diced into 1/2-inch pieces
2 cloves garlic, chopped
1/2 cup Basic Vinaigrette (see recipe, page 187)
1/2 cup hearts of palm, diced and minced
1/4 cup macadamia nuts, toasted and crushed

1. In sauté pan, heat oil over low heat.
2. Add mushrooms and cook until they are soft and any excess water has evaporated. Transfer to a bowl and set aside to cool.
3. Sauté onion and garlic until light brown.
4. Add onion and garlic to mushrooms.
5. Drizzle with Basic Vinaigrette and marinate for 4–36 hours.
6. Top with hearts of palm and macadamia nuts.
7. Serve warm or cold.

MAKES 2 SERVINGS.

PEAR BEET SALAD

POWER 2

1 cup pears, sliced
1/2 cup beets, sliced, steamed 15 minutes
1 1/2 cups leeks, sliced, steamed 10 minutes
2 tablespoons fresh arugula, chopped
1 tablespoon fresh fennel, chopped
1/4 cup olive oil
2 tablespoons prepared mustard
1 tablespoon fresh lemon juice
1/2 teaspoon cayenne pepper

1. In a large salad bowl, combine the pears, beets, leeks, arugula, and fennel.
2. In a separate bowl, whisk together olive oil, mustard, lemon juice, and cayenne pepper.
3. Add to salad and toss well.
4. Chill for 1 hour before serving.

MAKES 2 SERVINGS.

PEAR, JICAMA, AND PICKLE SALAD

POWER 2

2 firm pears, with skin, diced into 1/2-inch pieces
1 medium jicama, skinned, diced into 1/2-inch pieces
3 scallions, chopped lightly
1 yellow pepper, diced into 1/2-inch pieces
1 tablespoon mint, chopped lightly
1/4 teaspoon turmeric
1/4 cup mixed pickles, sliced
1 teaspoon sea salt
4 cups mixed baby salad greens
1/3 cup Basic Vinaigrette (see recipe, page 187)

1. In a large salad bowl, combine pears, jicama, scallions, pepper, mint, turmeric, sliced pickles, sea salt, and baby salad greens.
2. Drizzle with Basic Vinaigrette and toss well.
3. Serve immediately.

MAKES 4 SERVINGS.

POLYNESIAN SPROUT SALAD

POWER 3

coconut oil
2 cups whole walnuts, shelled
1/2 cup agave or other sweetener
2 cups red cabbage, sliced
1 cup raw carrots, diced
1 cup nori, sliced
2 cups sunflower sprouts
2 cups crunchy bean sprouts
1/2 cup toasted sesame seeds

1. Preheat oven to 375°F.
2. Lightly grease a cookie sheet with coconut oil. Coat the walnuts with agave and place on cookie sheet, and bake for 20 minutes.
3. In a large bowl, toss the red cabbage, carrots, nori, sprouts, and sesame seeds.
4. Toss the salad with your favorite dressing, and top with the walnuts.
5. Serve immediately.

MAKES 2 SERVINGS.

POTATO–GREEN BEAN SALAD

POWER 2

9 organic French fingerling
   potatoes or small red potatoes
2¹/₂ handfuls fresh string beans
¹/₄–¹/₃ cup olive oil
apple cider vinegar, to taste
   (optional)
¹/₂ large lemon, squeezed for juice
3 cloves garlic, minced

¹/₈–¹/₄ teaspoon sea salt or Hain's
   veggie salt
black pepper, to taste
dash cayenne
2 tablespoons parsley, minced
1 tablespoon palm hearts, cut
   lengthwise (optional)

1. Boil potatoes 12–20 minutes until fork slides into them easily. Allow potatoes to cool completely.
2. Clean string beans and remove stems. Boil until cooked, but firm.
3. Arrange cooked potatoes around outside of a dish or platter and put uncut, cooked string beans in the center.
4. Season with a mixture of olive oil, vinegar (optional), lemon juice, garlic, salt, and pepper.
5. Sprinkle cayenne and parsley over palm hearts and place in center.
6. Serve hot or cold.

MAKES 4–6 SERVINGS.

VERSION II

1. Follow cooking instructions as above, but be sure both potatoes and beans are well cooked, until soft.
2. Cut potatoes and green beans in small pieces and serve over salad greens.
3. Season with olive oil, lemon juice, garlic, salt, pepper, and dash of cayenne, to taste.
4. Serve hot or cold.

MAKES 4–6 SERVINGS.

POWER-FILLED WALDORF SALAD

POWER 1

¹/₂ lemon (1 tablespoon juice)
¹/₂ lime (1 tablespoon juice)
2 cups apples, unpeeled, diced
2 cups oranges, peeled and diced
1 cup celery, diced
1 cup unsalted walnuts, halved
¹/₂ cup blackberries
¹/₂ cup cherries, halved
¹/₂ cup soy mayonnaise
1 cup mixed baby salad greens

1. Separately push the lemon and lime through the juicer.
2. Set aside 1 tablespoon of the juice from each.
3. In a medium-size mixing bowl, combine the lemon and lime juices with the apples, oranges, celery, walnuts, blackberries, cherries, and soy mayonnaise, and mix well.
4. Serve on a bed of mixed baby salad greens, chilled or at room temperature.

MAKES 2 SERVINGS.

ROMAINE HEARTS–SPROUT SALAD

POWER 3

1 cup romaine hearts lettuce, sliced
1½ cups sunflower or bean sprouts
½ cup radicchio, sliced
¾ cup fresh tomato, chopped
½ cup cucumber, sliced
½ cup carrots, sliced
2 tablespoons radish, sliced
2 tablespoons fresh rosemary, chopped
2 tablespoons fresh basil, chopped
¼ cup white mushroom, sliced
¼ cup crunchy sprouts
¼ cup spicy sprouts
Basic Vinaigrette (see recipe, page 187)

1. Combine the lettuce, sunflower or bean sprouts, radicchio, tomato, cucumber, carrots, radish, rosemary, basil, and mushroom in a large salad bowl.
2. Top with crunchy and spicy sprouts and toss with the vinaigrette dressing.
3. Chill for 1 hour before serving.

MAKES 2 SERVINGS.

SESAME BEAN SALAD

POWER 3

¹/₂ cup white beans (canned)
¹/₂ cup black beans (canned)
¹/₂ cup kidney beans (canned)
¹/₄ cup scallions, sliced
1 cup orange segments, peeled and seeded
3 tablespoons orange juice
4¹/₂ teaspoons fresh lemon juice
¹/₄ cup toasted sesame oil
¹/₂ cup plus 3 tablespoons toasted sesame seeds
1¹/₂ teaspoons salt
¹/₂ teaspoon black pepper, freshly ground
¹/₄ teaspoon turmeric

1. In a large salad bowl, combine all beans, scallions, orange segments, orange juice, lemon juice, and sesame oil.
2. Sprinkle with sesame seeds and season with salt, pepper, and turmeric.
3. Mix well and chill for 1 hour before serving.

MAKES 2 SERVINGS.

SPICY ARUGULA-ENDIVE SALAD

POWER 3

1 cup beets, shredded
2 cups endive
1 cup baby arugula
1 cup yellow pepper, sliced
1 cup spicy sprouts
3/4 cup fresh Italian parsley, chopped
2/3 cup red cabbage, shredded
dash cayenne pepper
1 cup fresh tomatoes, diced, as garnish (optional)

1. Steam beets 1 minute.
2. In a large salad bowl, combine beets, endive, arugula, pepper, sprouts, parsley, cabbage, and cayenne, and toss thoroughly.
3. Garnish with diced tomatoes, if desired.
4. Serve with a strong lemon or vinaigrette dressing.

MAKES 2 SERVINGS.

SWISS CHARD AND RED POTATOES

POWER 5

1 tablespoon olive oil
1 leek, chopped
½ onion, peeled and chopped
1 clove elephant garlic or 3 regular cloves, chopped
2 cups Swiss chard, chopped
1 cup arugula, chopped
1 tablespoon fresh watercress, finely chopped
⅛ teaspoon powdered basil
2 russet potatoes, peeled and cubed
1 sweet potato, chopped
½ cup soymilk or rice milk powder with ¼ cup potato water (see below)
paprika, as garnish (optional)

1. In a sauté pan, heat the oil over medium heat.
2. Sauté the leek, onion, and garlic until soft, approximately 8–10 minutes.
3. Add chard, arugula, and watercress. Cover and cook until tender, stirring frequently, approximately 15–20 minutes.
4. In salted water, add basil and boil potatoes until they slide off a fork.
5. Drain, reserving ¼ cup cooking water.
6. Place the potatoes in a medium-size bowl, and add the sautéed greens. Slowly add the reconstituted rice milk or soymilk, and mash until moderately thick.
7. Garnish with a sprinkle of paprika, if desired.
8. Serve immediately.

MAKES 2 SERVINGS.

TASTY THAI SALAD

POWER 4

1 cup bean threads
10 mint leaves
1 cup sweet onion
2 scallions, tops included, chopped
¼ cucumber, thinly sliced
1 cup chickpeas, cooked
4 ounces firm tofu
1 tablespoon fresh parsley, chopped
1 stalk lemongrass, thinly sliced
⅛ teaspoon allspice
3 teaspoons agave or other sweetener
⅛ cup fresh lime juice
1 teaspoon rice vinegar
2 red chili peppers, seeded and chopped
1 tablespoon fresh mustard
1 small Boston lettuce
radish slices, as garnish (optional)

1. Cover bean threads in warm water and soak for 15 minutes. Drain and slice into thin, 3-inch strips.
2. In a bowl, combine bean threads, mint leaves, onion, scallions, cucumber, chickpeas, tofu, parsley, lemongrass, allspice, agave, lime juice, rice vinegar, red peppers, and mustard.
3. Line a salad bowl with Boston lettuce leaves, and spoon salad mixture into center.
4. Garnish with radish slices, if desired.
5. Serve immediately.

MAKES 6–8 SERVINGS.

THREE-BEAN VINAIGRETTE

POWER 4

1/2 cup pinto beans, cooked
1/2 cup kidney beans (canned), drained
1/2 cup green beans, steamed 15 minutes
1/2 cup yellow bell pepper, chopped
1/4 cup fresh watercress, chopped
1/4 cup hearts of palm
2 tablespoons red onion, chopped
2 tablespoons olive oil
2 tablespoons lemon juice
1–2 tablespoons prepared mustard
1–2 tablespoons apple cider vinegar
1/4 teaspoon black pepper, freshly ground

1. In a medium-size bowl, combine pinto beans, kidney beans, green beans, yellow pepper, watercress, hearts of palm, and onion.
2. In a small bowl, whisk together olive oil, lemon juice, mustard, vinegar, and pepper.
3. Pour dressing over bean mixture and toss thoroughly.
4. Chill before serving.

MAKES 2 SERVINGS.

TOFU AND BEAN SALAD

POWER 2

1 cup firm tofu, cubed
1 cup kidney beans (canned)
1/2 cup radishes, diced, steamed 15 minutes
1/2 cup daikon, diced
3/4 cup fennel, diced
1/3 cup olive oil
2–3 tablespoons apple cider or balsamic vinegar
2 tablespoons fresh basil, chopped, or dried basil
1 1/4 teaspoons prepared mustard
1/8 teaspoon dill seeds or leaves

1. In a large salad bowl, combine tofu, beans, radishes, daikon, fennel, olive oil, cider or balsamic vinegar, basil, mustard, and dill seeds or leaves, and toss thoroughly.
2. Chill for 1–2 hours before serving.

MAKES 2 SERVINGS.

TOMATO SALSA–RICE–AND–PASTA SALAD

POWER 2

12-ounce bag rice pasta, cooked (bow ties or penne)
5 cups broccoli florets, steamed
3 cups tomato salsa (1 jar spicy tomato salsa)
3 tomatoes, cooked
1½ cups cauliflower crowns, steamed
1 cup whole walnuts, toasted or sautéed
¾ cup red or yellow pepper, seeded and diced
¼ teaspoon salt
dash cayenne pepper, to taste

1. In a large mixing bowl, toss the pasta with the broccoli, salsa, tomatoes, cauliflower, walnuts, pepper, salt, and cayenne.
2. Serve cold as a main dish or a salad.

MAKES 4 SERVINGS.

WAKAME-DAIKON SALAD

*¹/₃ cup wakame, with tough stems removed, soaked for 15 minutes and
    drained*
¹/₄ cup pickling cucumbers, thinly sliced
¹/₄ cup lotus root, thinly sliced
¹/₄ cup daikon, shredded
2 tablespoons mustard
¹/₂–1 tablespoon balsamic vinegar
2 tablespoons lemon juice
2 tablespoons black sesame seeds

1. In a large salad bowl, combine the wakame, cucumbers, lotus
   root, daikon, and mustard.
2. Add vinegar and lemon juice and toss well.
3. Sprinkle with sesame seeds.
4. Serve immediately.

MAKES 2 SERVINGS.

WATERCRESS, ORANGE, AND ENDIVE SALAD

POWER 6

1 cup red, yellow, and orange bell peppers, sliced
1 cup endive, chopped
2 seedless oranges, sliced
1 cup sunflower sprouts
2/3 cup carrots, shredded
1 cup watercress
3/4 cup fresh Italian parsley, chopped
1 cup fresh yellow tomatoes, chopped, as garnish (optional)

1. In a large salad bowl, combine peppers, endive, oranges, sprouts, carrots, watercress, and parsley.
2. Garnish with chopped tomatoes, if desired.
3. Serve with a vinaigrette or light lemon dressing.

MAKES 2 SERVINGS.

YUKON GOLD POTATO SALAD

POWER 1

2 cups Yukon Gold potatoes, diced
1/2 cup celery, chopped
4 tablespoons sweet onion, chopped
2 tablespoons olive oil
1/8–1/4 cup vegan mayonnaise
1 tablespoon sweet relish
2 teaspoons fresh dill, chopped
1 teaspoon celery seeds
1 teaspoon lemon juice
1 teaspoon flaxseed oil
1 teaspoon sea salt
1/2 teaspoon black pepper

1. Steam potatoes for 25 minutes until cooked but firm. Allow potatoes to cool completely.
2. In a medium-size mixing bowl, toss together potatoes, celery, onion, oil, mayonnaise, relish, dill, celery seeds, lemon juice, and flaxseed oil.
3. Season with salt and pepper, and mix thoroughly.
4. Serve cold or at room temperature.

MAKES 2 SERVINGS.

YUMMY POTATO SALAD

POWER 3

4 purple potatoes
½ cup sweet onion, diced
½ cup apple cider vinegar
¼ cup olive oil
¼ cup fresh arugula, chopped
2 tablespoons fresh basil, chopped
2 tablespoons prepared mustard
1 tablespoon fresh dill, chopped
1 teaspoon ginger, grated
½ teaspoon salt
¼ teaspoon black pepper, freshly ground

1. Steam potatoes 15–20 minutes, until tender. Allow to cool completely, then slice.
2. In a medium-size bowl, toss together potatoes, onion, vinegar, oil, arugula, basil, mustard, dill, and ginger.
3. Season with salt and pepper.
4. Serve at room temperature or chilled.

MAKES 2 SERVINGS.

Chapter Eight

SIDE DISHES

BRAISED ENDIVE

POWER 2

4 endives
¹/₂ tablespoon olive oil
¹/₂ tablespoon toasted sesame oil
1 teaspoon sea salt
black pepper, freshly ground
1 tablespoon agave or other sweetener
¹/₂ tablespoon fresh lemon juice
¹/₂ teaspoon lime juice
1 tablespoon water
2 tablespoons sweet onion, chopped, as garnish (optional)

1. Preheat oven to 350°F.
2. Trim and core the endives.
3. Moisten a paper towel with olive oil and oil the bottom and sides of an ovenproof dish. Put the whole endives in the dish.

4. Sprinkle endives with toasted sesame oil, sea salt, pepper, agave, lemon and lime juices, and water.
5. Cover with aluminum foil and bake until endives are tender, approximately 50 minutes.
6. Garnish with chopped onion, if desired.
7. Serve immediately.

MAKES 4 SERVINGS.

BROCCOLI WILD RICE

POWER 2

2 cups wild and brown rice
1/2 cup broccoli florets, steamed 5–8 minutes
1/2 cup shiitake mushrooms, sliced
1/4 cup green olives, sliced
3 tablespoons apple cider vinegar
1 tablespoon tamari
1 tablespoon soy sauce
pinch cayenne
pinch red chili pepper
1/2 cup hearts of palm, sliced, as garnish (optional)
1/2 cup marinated sun-dried tomatoes, as garnish (optional)

1. Cook rice according to directions on package.
2. In medium-size bowl, combine rice, steamed broccoli, shiitake mushrooms, and olives.
3. In a separate bowl, whisk together cider vinegar, tamari, soy sauce, cayenne, and chili pepper.
4. Pour dressing over rice and vegetable mixture, and toss well.
5. Refrigerate for 2 hours before serving.
6. Garnish with sliced hearts of palm and marinated sun-dried tomatoes, if desired.
7. Serve chilled.

MAKES 2 SERVINGS.

CAULIFLOWER AND GARLIC IN CURRY

POWER 3

1/8 cup apple cider vinegar
1/4 cup rice syrup
1/2 cup water
2 teaspoons Madras Curry Powder
2 potatoes, peeled, cubed, and boiled
2 yellow onions, peeled, sliced into 1/2-inch pieces
1 head cauliflower, core removed, cut into florets
2 teaspoons raisins
2 tablespoons dried blueberries
2 tablespoons dried cherries
2 tablespoons olive oil
8 cloves garlic, peeled and diced
1/2 teaspoon turmeric

1. In a saucepan, bring vinegar, rice syrup, and water to a simmer.
2. Add curry powder, potatoes, onions, cauliflower, raisins, blueberries, and cherries, and continue to simmer, covered, for 2 minutes.
3. In a separate pan, heat oil and sauté garlic and turmeric until light brown, and add to the above mixture.
4. Allow to sit at room temperature for 1 hour, then chill in refrigerator before serving.

MAKES 4 SERVINGS.

FAMILY-STYLE GARLIC
MASHED POTATOES

POWER 2

8 potatoes, washed and peeled (peels can be left on as a variation)
8 cloves garlic, 2 minced and set aside
1 cup soymilk
1/2 cup olive oil
2 teaspoons sea salt, or to taste
1 teaspoon cayenne, or to taste
1/2 teaspoon paprika

1. Place potatoes and 6 cloves of garlic in a large pot and cover with water. Bring to a boil and cook, uncovered, until potatoes are very tender, 20–30 minutes.
2. Remove from heat and drain off most of the water. Mash potatoes with potato masher.
3. Return pot to stove on low heat and add soymilk, olive oil, minced garlic, salt, cayenne, and paprika, and blend until fluffy.
4. If potatoes are not fluffy or moist enough, add more soymilk and olive oil.
5. Serve immediately.

MAKES 4 SERVINGS.

GARLIC YUKON MASHED POTATOES WITH SHIITAKE MUSHROOM SAUCE

POWER 4

1 pound medium Yukon Gold
*   potatoes*
3 tablespoons olive oil
1 cup fresh basil
1 teaspoon rosemary
dash cayenne pepper
¼ cup plain soymilk
1 teaspoon salt
white pepper, freshly ground, to
*   taste*

MUSHROOM SAUCE:
1 tablespoon olive oil
1 teaspoon garlic, chopped
¼ cup onion, diced into ¼-inch
*   pieces*
1½ cups shiitake mushrooms
1 teaspoon tarragon, chopped
1 teaspoon salt

FOR THE POTATOES:

1. Wash and halve the potatoes.
2. Place potatoes in a pot of cold water with olive oil, basil, rosemary, and cayenne. Bring to a simmer and cook for approximately 30 minutes, or until you can insert a knife easily into a potato.
3. Drain potatoes and pass them through a ricer.
4. Add soymilk, salt, and pepper, and mash with a potato masher.

FOR THE SAUCE:

1. In a saucepan, heat oil on low.
2. Cook garlic and onion until lightly brown. Add mushrooms and cook on low for 15 minutes.
3. Stir in tarragon and salt.
4. Pour sauce over potatoes.
5. Serve immediately.

MAKES 2 SERVINGS.

GARY'S FAVORITE POTATOES

POWER 1

1¾ teaspoons olive oil (divided into ¼ teaspoon and 1½ teaspoons)
2 large russet potatoes, halved lengthwise
10 shiitake mushrooms, with stems removed, washed and halved
dash cayenne pepper
dash sea salt
dash black pepper
parsley, as garnish (optional)

1. Preheat oven to 475°F.
2. Coat baking dish with ¼ teaspoon of olive oil. Place potatoes in oiled baking dish, skin side down. Bake potatoes 45 minutes to an hour, or until soft.
3. In a sauté pan, heat 1½ teaspoons olive oil and sauté mushrooms for 5 minutes.
4. Add cayenne pepper, salt, and black pepper to taste.
5. Arrange sautéed mushrooms down center of baked potatoes and garnish with parsley, if desired.
6. Serve immediately.

MAKES 2 SERVINGS.

HASH PURPLE POTATOES WITH GARLIC

POWER 3

²/₃ cup olive oil (¹/₃ cup for vegetables, ¹/₃ cup for potatoes)
2 cloves garlic, peeled and mashed
1 portobello mushroom cap, washed
¹/₂ cup yellow pepper, diced
1 onion, peeled, diced
2 cups whole basil leaves
2 pounds purple potatoes, washed, grated
dash Tabasco sauce
dash cayenne pepper
1 teaspoon salt
¹/₄ teaspoon black pepper

1. In ¹/₃ cup olive oil, sauté garlic, mushroom, yellow pepper, onion, and basil over medium heat for 8 minutes.
2. In ¹/₃ cup olive oil, stir-fry potatoes over medium heat, until crisp.
3. Toss fried potatoes with sautéed vegetables, Tabasco sauce and cayenne, and sprinkle with salt and black pepper.
4. Serve immediately.

MAKES 4 SERVINGS.

HEALTHY HIJIKI

POWER 2

2 tablespoons toasted sesame oil
1 cup hijiki, soaked in water and drained
2 tablespoons scallions, finely chopped
2 tablespoons red bell pepper, diced
1 tablespoon tamari

1. In a large skillet, heat sesame oil.
2. Sauté the hijiki, scallions, pepper, and tamari in the skillet over medium heat for 5 minutes.
3. Serve at room temperature. This can be stored for up to 2 days in a refrigerator and served cold.

MAKES 2 SERVINGS.

JAPANESE BUTTERNUT SQUASH WITH TOASTED SESAME SAUCE

1 butternut squash
2 tablespoons toasted sesame oil
6–8 tablespoons tahini
3–4 tablespoons gomasio

1. Steam the whole squash for 30 minutes or until you can stick a knife into it with no resistance.
2. Remove from heat, let cool for 10 minutes, and slice into ½-inch pieces.
3. In a small bowl, combine the oil and tahini, and mix well.
4. Pour the dressing over the squash and sprinkle with gomasio.
5. Serve immediately.

MAKES 2–3 SERVINGS.

KOMBU SEAWEED WITH TOASTED SESAME

POWER 3

8 ounces kombu seaweed
1/2 cup bell pepper, diced into 1/2-inch pieces
1/2 cup sweet onion, diced into 1/2-inch pieces
3 scallions, sliced
3 tablespoons rice syrup
2 tablespoons toasted sesame oil
2 tablespoons olive oil
1 teaspoon ginger
1 teaspoon sesame seeds

1. Cook seaweed in water for 25 minutes, then drain and cool.
2. Add pepper, onion, and scallions to cooked seaweed.
3. In a small bowl, whisk together rice syrup, sesame oil, olive oil, and ginger.
4. Pour dressing over salad and toss well.
5. Top with sesame seeds.
6. Serve immediately.

MAKES 4 SERVINGS.

NEW SOUTHERN GREENS

POWER 2

3 cups Basic Vegetable Stock (see recipe, page 154)
2 bunches of greens (collard, chard, kale, mustard, turnip, or mixture)
1 large tomato, cubed
⅓ cup pine nuts
½ cup black olives, deli style
2 teaspoons olive oil

1. Bring stock to a simmer.
2. Add greens and cook until tender, but not overdone (15–20 minutes).
3. Remove greens from heat and add tomato, pine nuts, and olives.
4. Drizzle olive oil over the mix, and toss well.
5. Serve immediately.

MAKES 3–4 SERVINGS.

ROASTED ROOT VEGETABLES

POWER 4

1 turnip, peeled and quartered
1 carrot, not peeled, quartered
1 parsnip, cored and quartered
8 pearl onions, peeled
4 Russian fingerlings, halved
4 Yukon Gold potatoes, halved
2 shallots, peeled
4 cloves garlic, peeled
*1 small celery root, peeled, diced
    into 1-inch pieces*

¹/₄ cup agave or other sweetener
¹/₂ cup balsamic vinegar
¹/₈ cup rice vinegar
1 teaspoon mirin
1 teaspoon basil
¹/₂ teaspoon salt
¹/₂ teaspoon coarse black pepper
dash cayenne pepper
2 tablespoons toasted sesame seeds

1. Preheat oven to 300°F.
2. In a large baking pan, roast turnip, carrot, parsnip, onions, potatoes, shallots, garlic, and celery root for 30–45 minutes, or until thoroughly cooked.*
3. Transfer roasted vegetables to a large bowl.
4. In a small bowl, whisk agave, balsamic and rice vinegars, mirin, basil, salt, pepper, and a dash of cayenne.
5. Pour dressing over vegetables in bowl and toss until well coated.
6. Return vegetables to pan and bake for 10 more minutes.
7. Remove from oven and sprinkle with toasted sesame seeds.
8. Serve immediately.

MAKES 3 SERVINGS.

*__Chef's Note:__ Adding leeks and sweet onions halfway into the baking process is a tasty variation.

SAUTÉED KALE WITH SHIITAKE MUSHROOMS

POWER 2

3 teaspoons toasted sesame oil
1 teaspoon soy sauce
2 cups kale, washed and sliced
2 cups shiitake mushrooms, stemmed and sliced
1 tablespoon agave or other sweetener
1 teaspoon tarragon, chopped

1. In a large skillet, heat sesame oil and soy sauce.
2. Add kale and shiitake mushrooms and sauté over medium heat for 10 minutes.
3. Remove from heat and toss with agave and tarragon.
4. Serve immediately.

MAKES 2 SERVINGS.

SAVORY BUTTERNUT SQUASH

1 *butternut squash, halved*
4 *tablespoons Earth Balance (dairy-free buttery spread)*
2 *tablespoons rice syrup*
2 *tablespoons agave or other sweetener*
½ teaspoon cinnamon
¼ teaspoon nutmeg (optional)
pinch salt
1 *teaspoon hazelnut oil*

1. Preheat oven to 350°F.
2. Place squash in a baking pan with enough water to cover bottom of pan, and bake for 40 minutes.
3. In a small bowl, mix the Earth Balance, rice syrup, agave, cinnamon, nutmeg, salt, and hazelnut oil until smooth.
4. Pour the sauce mixture over the squash and bake 5–15 minutes longer, or until squash is tender.
5. Serve immediately.

MAKES 2 SERVINGS.

STICKY BLACK SWEET RICE ON MANGO

POWER 1

2¹/₄ cups coconut milk
¹/₃ cup agave or other sweetener
¹/₄ teaspoon sea salt
1 cup short-grain brown rice, rinsed
4 tablespoons raisins
2 tablespoons pine nuts
2 ripe mangos, seeded, sliced
1 teaspoon fresh lemon juice
¹/₄ cup blueberries
thick coconut cream (optional)
2 mint leaves, as garnish (optional)

1. In a large saucepan, bring coconut milk and agave to a boil, then add salt and cook for 5 minutes.
2. Add rice, stir, and reduce heat to simmer, covered.
3. Check after 20 minutes. Remove from heat when all liquid has been absorbed.
4. Mix raisins and pine nuts into rice mixture.
5. Sprinkle mango slices with lemon juice and top with rice mixture and blueberries. Add a dollop of coconut cream, if desired.
6. Garnish with one mint leaf, if desired.
7. Serve immediately.

MAKES 2 SERVINGS.

STUFFED POTATOES WITH
PINTO BEANS AND SOY CHEESE

POWER 3

2 Idaho potatoes, baked, then halved, with center taken out and skins
   set aside
1/2 teaspoon paprika
1 teaspoon salt
2 tablespoons sweet onion, chopped
1/2 teaspoon black pepper, freshly ground
2 tablespoons fresh parsley, chopped
1 cup soy cheese, shredded (optional)
1 cup pinto beans, mashed
2–3 tablespoons olive oil
1/4 teaspoon cayenne pepper

1. Preheat oven to 425°F.
2. In a large bowl, mash the insides of the potatoes and mix with
   paprika, salt, sweet onion, black pepper, chopped parsley, soy
   cheese, pinto beans, olive oil, and cayenne pepper.
3. Stuff the mixture back into the skins, and return to oven for
   10 minutes, or until tops are browned.
4. Serve immediately.

MAKES 2 SERVINGS.

SUCCULENT CRANBERRY SAUCE

3 cups water
1 16-ounce package cranberries
1/2 cup agave or other sweetener
4 tablespoons agar-agar
1/2 teaspoon orange extract
1/4 teaspoon almond extract
1/4 teaspoon lemon extract
1/8 teaspoon maple extract
dash stevia

1. Bring water and cranberries to a boil, stirring frequently.
2. Keep heat on high until cranberries start to pop, about 5–10 minutes.
3. Lower heat to medium and add agave, agar-agar, orange, almond, lemon, and maple extracts, and stevia.
4. Mix well and continue to stir as mixture thickens slightly.
5. Turn off heat and allow mixture to cool for 3–5 minutes.
6. Pour into Pyrex dish and refrigerate before serving.

MAKES 4 SERVINGS.

SWEET AND SOUR SAFFRON RICE

POWER 4

2 tablespoons olive oil
1 sweet red pepper, sliced thinly
1 sweet yellow pepper, sliced thinly
1 medium onion, chopped
2 cloves garlic, minced
2 cups basmati rice
3 cups boiling water
pinch saffron
1 teaspoon sea salt
1/2 cup peas, cooked
2 tablespoons coconut oil (or macadamia nut or palm)
3 tablespoons tamari
1/4 cup shiitake mushrooms

1. In a saucepan, heat oil and sauté peppers, onion, and garlic until soft.
2. Add rice and stir until grains are coated with oil.
3. Add boiling water, saffron, and salt. Cover and simmer for approximately 20 minutes, until rice is cooked and all the water is absorbed.
4. Add peas and fluff with a fork.
5. In a skillet, heat coconut oil and tamari and sauté mushrooms for 5 minutes on high heat.
6. Pour mushrooms over rice.
7. Serve warm.

MAKES 2 SERVINGS.

SWEET MUSTARD WITH BOK CHOY

POWER 2

2 tablespoons toasted sesame oil
1 teaspoon soy sauce
2 cloves garlic, crushed
2 heads baby bok choy, sliced
1/4 cup mustard
2 teaspoons agave or other sweetener
2 tablespoons lemongrass, chopped
1/2 teaspoon cardamom
1/2 teaspoon anise

1. In a saucepan, heat sesame oil and soy sauce and sauté garlic until tender.
2. Steam bok choy for 5 minutes.
3. Add the bok choy, mustard, agave, lemongrass, cardamom, and anise to the sautéed garlic, and cook for 3 minutes over medium heat.
4. Serve hot.

MAKES 1 SERVING.

TANGY TOMATO PILAF

POWER 4

4 tablespoons olive oil
1 large onion, diced
2 cloves garlic, minced
1 jalapeño pepper, diced
2 small or 1 large tomato (approximately 8 ounces), chopped
2 tablespoons fresh basil, chopped
½ teaspoon parsley
¼ teaspoon dried fennel
1 cup white basmati rice, cooked
1¼ cups vegetable broth
pinch saffron
pinch cayenne
sea salt, to taste
2 tablespoons almonds, sliced, as garnish (optional)
fresh greens for decoration (optional)

1. In a saucepan, heat the oil over moderate heat and sauté the onion, garlic, and jalapeño pepper for about 3 minutes, or until onion is translucent.
2. Add tomato, basil, parsley, and fennel, and sauté 5 minutes.
3. Add rice, vegetable broth, saffron, cayenne, and sea salt. Bring to a boil, then reduce to a simmer. Cover and cook for 5 minutes.
4. Remove from heat. Remove lid, and cover with a cloth towel to allow evaporation of excess water vapor without loss of heat. Let stand 10 minutes.
5. Garnish with sliced almonds and serve on a bed of fresh greens or as a vegetable stuffing, if desired.
6. Serve immediately.

MAKES 2 SERVINGS.

TASTY POTATO PANCAKES

POWER 1

4 new potatoes, peeled
1/2 cup rice milk or soymilk
1/4 cup egg substitute
3 tablespoons agave or other sweetener
3 tablespoons brown rice flour
1/8 teaspoon sea salt
1/4 teaspoon cinnamon
4 tablespoons coconut oil

1. Boil potatoes until tender, and then mash them.
2. Add rice milk or soymilk, egg substitute, agave, brown rice flour, salt, and cinnamon to mashed potatoes.
3. Shape mashed potatoes into cakes.
4. In a sauté pan, heat coconut oil over medium-high heat and sauté potato cakes until golden brown.
5. Serve immediately.

MAKES 2 SERVINGS.

THREE-ALARM POTATOES

POWER 3

1 pound russet potatoes
2 tablespoons coconut oil
1 teaspoon cumin
1 ripe tomato, peeled and chopped, about ¼ cup
½ teaspoon cayenne
½ teaspoon turmeric
1 tablespoon agave or other sweetener
1 tablespoon soy yogurt
½ teaspoon fresh ginger, ground
½ tablespoon cloves, ground
½ tablespoon dried tarragon
½ tablespoon fresh basil, chopped
black pepper, freshly ground, to taste
1 teaspoon sea salt
¼ cup water

1. Boil whole potatoes, skins on, until almost soft. Allow potatoes to cool completely and peel.
2. In a skillet, heat the oil over moderate heat and brown whole potatoes for 3 minutes per side. Remove potatoes from oil and set aside. Discard all but 1 teaspoon oil.
3. In the skillet, heat the remaining oil over moderate heat and stir-fry cumin for 10 seconds.
4. Add tomato, cayenne, turmeric, and agave, and stir-fry for 2 minutes.
5. Add soy yogurt, ginger, cloves, tarragon, basil, and pepper, and continue to stir-fry for 3 minutes.
6. Add whole potatoes, salt, and water, and simmer, covered, over low heat, until water evaporates and a thick sauce remains.
7. Serve immediately.

MAKES 2 SERVINGS.

WILTED ARUGULA WITH
OYSTER MUSHROOMS AND SOY PARMESAN

POWER 2

¼ cup extra-virgin olive oil
2 cups oyster mushrooms, stemmed
2–3¼ tablespoons fresh mint, chopped
1 tablespoon soy sauce
1 teaspoon salt
5 cups arugula
1 teaspoon soy Parmesan cheese, grated
⅛ teaspoon black pepper, freshly ground

1. In a large saucepan, heat oil and sauté the mushrooms, mint, soy sauce, and salt over medium heat, uncovered, for 3–4 minutes, being careful not to overcook.
2. Turn off the heat and place the arugula leaves on top of the mushroom mixture. Cover pan for 1 minute to wilt the leaves.
3. Turn out onto a large platter and sprinkle with cheese and pepper.
4. Serve warm.

MAKES 2 SERVINGS.

Chapter Nine

ENTRÉES

ACORN SQUASH BAKE

POWER 3

1 acorn squash, halved and seeded
½ cup yellow pepper, minced
½ cup papaya, cubed
¼ cup crunchy sprouts
¼ cup tomato, cubed

⅛ cup Vidalia onion, minced
pinch salt and pepper
olive oil to drizzle on squash
handful of walnuts or pecans (raw)

1. Preheat oven to 325°F.
2. Place squash skin side up on cooking sheet and bake for 25–35 minutes, until soft (when fork easily punctures squash). Set baked squash aside and allow to cool.
3. Mix together pepper, papaya, sprouts, tomato, onion, salt, and pepper.
4. Scoop out a small portion of the squash and fill with mixed ingredients.
5. Drizzle with olive oil and top with nuts.
6. Serve immediately.

MAKES 2 SERVINGS.

ALGERIAN SPICY TOFU CHILI

POWER 7

2 cups dried kidney beans
1/8 cup extra-virgin olive oil
1 onion, finely chopped
1 scallion, finely chopped
1 1/2 small dried red chilies
10 cloves garlic, minced
1/2 tablespoon sweet paprika
1/8 teaspoon black pepper, freshly
   ground
1 tablespoon green bell pepper,
   minced
1 tablespoon curry powder

2 teaspoons ground cumin
15 sun-dried tomatoes,
   reconstituted and puréed for
   1/2 cup tomato paste
1 tomato, coarsely chopped
3 1/2 cups water or vegetable broth
1 pound firm tofu, diced in
   1/2-inch cubes
pinch cayenne
2 teaspoons sea salt, to taste
1 cup arugula, chopped
5 fresh watercress sprigs, chopped

1. Soak the dried beans overnight in 32 ounces of water, covered. Drain and set aside.
2. In a large soup pot, heat the oil over medium heat and cook the onion and scallion, stirring occasionally, until tender, 6–8 minutes.
3. Add the chilies, garlic, paprika, black pepper, green pepper, curry powder, and cumin. Cook, stirring, for 2–3 minutes.
4. Add the sun-dried tomato paste and cook 1–2 minutes, stirring, until the mixture thickens. Stir in the fresh tomato and 1 cup of the water or broth, and bring to a boil.
5. Add the beans, diced tofu, and the remaining 2 1/2 cups water or broth, cayenne, and salt.
6. Lower the heat to medium-low, cover, and cook until the beans are tender, 1–2 hours.
7. Discard the chilies before serving. Stir in the arugula and watercress.
8. Serve warm.

MAKES 4–6 SERVINGS.

AROMATIC THAI RICE

POWER 1

5 teaspoons toasted peanut oil
¼ cup zucchini, chopped
1 cup yellow onions, chopped
½ teaspoon shallots, chopped
3 cups long-grain brown rice, cooked
¼ cup unsalted roasted peanuts, chopped
½ cup macadamia nuts, roasted
5 artichoke hearts
¼ cup water chestnuts (canned)
3 teaspoons garlic, chopped
4½ teaspoons fresh mint, chopped, as garnish (optional)

1. In a skillet or wok, heat the peanut oil over high heat until hot but not smoking.
2. Add the zucchini, onions, and shallots, and sauté over medium heat for 5 minutes.
3. Stir in the rice, peanuts, macadamia nuts, artichoke hearts, water chestnuts, and garlic, and cook until hot.
4. Garnish with chopped mint, if desired.
5. Serve immediately.

MAKES 4 SERVINGS.

ASIAN RICE NOODLES

POWER 4

3 cups carrots, thinly sliced into matchsticks
¼ cup toasted sesame oil
3½ cups shiitake mushrooms, stemmed and sliced
1 cup scallions, sliced
½ teaspoon fresh ginger, grated
6 ounces dry rice sticks (rice noodles)
½ cup plus 1 tablespoon tamari
4 cups water
2 teaspoons arrowroot
2 cups sugar snap peas

1. Steam carrot matchsticks for 10 minutes.
2. In a large saucepan, heat the oil over medium-high heat and sauté the carrot sticks, mushrooms, scallions, and ginger for 2–3 minutes.
3. Add the noodles, tamari, water, and arrowroot. Cook another 3–5 minutes, stirring everything together.
4. Remove from heat and add sugar snap peas.
5. Let stand, covered, for 10 minutes before serving.

MAKES 4 SERVINGS.

BABY LIMA BEAN AND MUSHROOM SAUTÉ

POWER 3

2 tablespoons olive oil
1 cup mushrooms, sliced
1/2 cup onions, sliced
1 teaspoon salt
1 teaspoon garlic, minced
1/2 teaspoon fresh parsley, chopped
1 cup lima beans, cooked
1/2 cup millet, cooked

1. In a skillet, heat oil and sauté mushrooms and onions until onions are translucent.
2. Add salt, garlic, parsley, lima beans, and millet.
3. Mix well and serve warm.

MAKES 2 SERVINGS.

BASIC LENTILS AND RICE

POWER 3

2 tablespoons oil (sunflower, soy, or safflower)
½ cup carrots, sliced, cooked
¾ cup onions, chopped
¼ cup celery, sliced
1 teaspoon dried sage
1 cup lentils, cooked
1 cup long-grain brown rice, cooked
dash sea salt
dash black pepper

1. In a large saucepan, heat the oil over medium heat and sauté the carrots, onions, and celery with the sage until the onions are clear.
2. Add the lentils and rice and warm through.
3. Add salt and pepper to taste.
4. Serve hot.

MAKES 2–3 SERVINGS.

BASMATI WITH ARUGULA, OLIVES, AND PEARS

POWER 3

1 cup basmati rice, uncooked
4 cups arugula
1 cup distilled water
1/2 cup pears, diced
1/8 cup watercress, finely chopped
3/4 teaspoon fresh basil, finely chopped (or 1/2 teaspoon dried)
1/2 clove garlic, pressed
1 tablespoon roasted macadamia nuts, chopped
sea salt, to taste
black pepper, freshly ground, to taste
8 Greek olives, green and black, pitted and chopped
1 3/4 tablespoons olive oil
1 tablespoon balsamic vinegar
1/4 cup tempeh, crumbled
parsley, as garnish (optional)

1. Cook rice according to package directions.
2. Wash arugula leaves and steam until just wilted.
3. In a glass jar, mix water, pears, watercress, basil, garlic, macadamia nuts, salt, and pepper. Cover tightly and shake well.
4. In a bowl, combine rice and chopped olives. Pour olive oil and vinegar over mixture and toss.
5. Arrange steamed arugula leaves on 2 plates. Fill with rice and olive mixture and sprinkle tempeh on top.
6. Garnish with parsley, if desired.
7. Serve immediately.

MAKES 2 SERVINGS.

BEAN MOUNTAIN ON RICE

POWER 3

2 cups brown jasmine rice
1 16-ounce can organic black beans
8 sun-dried tomatoes, marinated
4 pieces arugula
4 slices cucumber
4 slices daikon
10 black olives
dash cayenne pepper
dash salt
dash black pepper
peanut or olive oil

1. Cook rice according to instructions on package (use peanut oil in place of butter).
2. Place cooked rice on a dish and add beans in center.
3. Arrange sun-dried tomatoes, arugula, cucumber slices, and daikon slices around edge of plate. Arrange black olives around edge of rice to form a border.
4. Season daikon slices with cayenne pepper, and cucumber slices with salt and pepper. Drizzle peanut oil or olive oil on cooked rice for added flavor.
5. Serve immediately.

MAKES 2 SERVINGS.

BLACK & GREEN OLIVE RATATOUILLE

POWER 3

1 tablespoon olive oil
1 onion, diced into 1-inch pieces
6 baby zucchini, diced into 1-inch pieces
1 yellow bell pepper, seeded and diced
1 eggplant, diced into 1-inch pieces
1 cup marinated sun-dried tomatoes, sliced
2 tomatoes, each diced into 1-inch pieces, juice saved
½ cup large green olives, pitted and halved
½ cup large black olives, pitted and halved
½ teaspoon rosemary, chopped
½ cup fresh fennel, chopped
2 cloves garlic, chopped
3 teaspoons basil, chopped
salt and pepper to taste
dash cayenne pepper
pine nuts or pineapple chunks, as garnish (optional)

1. In a large skillet, heat oil and sauté onion, zucchini, bell pepper, and eggplant on low heat until vegetables are soft.
2. Add tomatoes and olives and simmer for 10 minutes.
3. Add rosemary, fennel, garlic, and basil. Season with salt, pepper, and cayenne.
4. Garnish with pine nuts and/or pineapple chunks, if desired.
5. Serve immediately.

MAKES 4 SERVINGS.

BRAZILIAN BROCCOLI

POWER 3

1 cup broccoli florets, cut into bite-size pieces
1/2 cup snap beans, cut into bite-size pieces
1/2 cup kale, coarsely chopped
1 cup black beans, cooked
3 tablespoons Brazil nuts, chopped
2 tablespoons olive oil
1 teaspoon garlic, minced
1 tablespoon fresh chives
1 teaspoon salt
1/4 teaspoon tarragon

1. Steam broccoli, snap beans, and kale for 8 minutes, or until tender.
2. Combine with black beans, Brazil nuts, olive oil, garlic, chives, salt, and tarragon, and mix well.
3. Serve hot or cold.

MAKES 2 SERVINGS.

CAJUN TOFU

POWER 1

1 pound firm tofu
4 tablespoons Cajun seasoning (nonirradiated)
2 teaspoons olive oil
2 cups cooked brown rice

1. Slice tofu into four equal pieces. Let tofu drain, wrapped in towel, for 20 minutes.
2. Spread Cajun seasoning on a plate and cover one or both sides of tofu (depending on how spicy you like it).
3. In a nonstick skillet, heat olive oil over medium-high heat. Place tofu in skillet and sear each side, until a desired degree of color is reached.
4. Serve with brown rice.

MAKES 2 SERVINGS.

CAMBODIAN SOBA PEANUT NOODLES

POWER 4

7 *tablespoons toasted sesame oil*
1 *clove garlic*
¹/4 cup smooth peanut butter
4 *teaspoons pure maple syrup*
1 *teaspoon fresh lime juice*
¹/3 cup plus 1 tablespoon water
2 *drops hot chili oil or Tabasco sauce*
1 *cup yellow onions, diced*
1 *cup shiitake mushrooms, stemmed and sliced*
¹/2 cup scallions, sliced
¹/4 cup celery, diced
gomasio, to taste
4 *cups soba noodles, cooked*

1. In a blender, combine 1 tablespoon oil, garlic, peanut butter, maple syrup, lime juice, water, and hot chili oil or Tabasco sauce, and blend until smooth, 2–3 minutes. Set aside.
2. In a large saucepan, heat the remaining 6 tablespoons oil over medium heat, then sauté the onions, mushrooms, scallions, and celery for 8–10 minutes.
3. Remove from heat and stir in the peanut sauce and gomasio.
4. Toss the soba noodles with the vegetables and sauce in a large bowl, until all the noodles are covered.
5. Chill for 90 minutes before serving.

MAKES 2–4 SERVINGS.

CARIBBEAN SPICY RICE

POWER 4

2 cups brown short-grain basmati rice
1 parsnip, peeled and sliced
1 chayote
1½ cups pumpkin, canned or fresh
⅓ pound broad beans, soaked overnight
1 sweet red pepper, chopped
1 sweet potato, peeled and diced
2 scallions, including tops, chopped
2 large ripe tomatoes, cored and chopped
5 tablespoons olive oil
½ teaspoon cayenne pepper
¼ teaspoon dried fennel
sea salt, to taste
Boston or mesclun lettuce for garnish

1. Steam rice until just tender.
2. In a large pot, place parsnip, chayote, pumpkin, beans, sweet pepper, sweet potato, scallions, and tomatoes. Cover with water and cook over medium heat, until tender. Drain liquid.
3. Add 3 tablespoons of the olive oil, cayenne pepper, fennel, salt, and rice.
4. In a large nonstick pan, heat remaining 2 tablespoons of olive oil. Transfer the rice mixture into the pan. Cook on medium-low heat for 10 minutes.
5. Garnish with lettuce and serve hot.

MAKES 6 SERVINGS.

CHILI CON TEMPEH

POWER 7

2 16-ounce cans chopped tomatoes
1 3-ounce can tomato paste
1 cup frozen corn
1 zucchini, chopped
2 carrots, chopped
1 large onion, coarsely chopped
1 bell pepper, chopped
1 jalapeño pepper, minced
3 tablespoons chili powder, or more to taste
2 teaspoons cumin
2 teaspoons garlic powder
1 teaspoon dried oregano
1 package tempeh, crumbled
1 15-ounce can kidney, pinto, or black beans

1. In a large pot, combine tomatoes, tomato paste, corn, zucchini, carrots, onion, bell pepper, jalapeño pepper, chili powder, cumin, garlic powder, and oregano.
2. Cover and simmer for 1 hour.
3. Add the tempeh and beans and simmer for 30 minutes more.
4. Serve over brown rice or whole-grain pasta.

MAKES 4 SERVINGS.

CLAIRE AND CHRISTINA'S
STAFF HOUSE DINNER

POWER 6

5 tablespoons olive oil
2 cloves garlic, minced
3 cups onions, chopped
3 small zucchinis, cut lengthwise
1 cup baby carrots
5 cups greens, steamed
3 tablespoons parsley
Cajun seasoning, to taste
2 tablespoons tamari
2 tablespoons sherry
2 tablespoons mirin
1 package wild rice tempeh
1 tomato, cubed
5 avocado slices, as garnish

1. In a large saucepan, heat 2 tablespoons of the oil and sauté garlic.
2. Add onions and cook until they are translucent.
3. Gradually add the zucchinis, carrots, greens, and parsley with Cajun seasoning to taste, and cook until tender.
4. In a separate pan, heat the tamari, sherry, and mirin over medium-high heat. Add the tempeh and tomato to the skillet and cook for 15 minutes.
5. Spoon the tempeh and tomato mixture over the vegetables.
6. Top with avocado slices.
7. Drizzle remaining olive oil over the mix.
8. Serve immediately.

MAKES 4 SERVINGS.

CURRIED LENTILS WITH SESAME TOFU

POWER 3

6 cups water
1 cup French lentils, sorted and rinsed
2 teaspoons curry powder
4 teaspoons toasted sesame oil
1/2 medium onion, diced into 1/4-inch pieces
1 cup tofu, sliced (marinated overnight with 12 ounces of soy sauce,
  miso, and agave syrup)
1/2 cup raisins
2 pears, diced into 1/4-inch pieces
1 tablespoon apple cider vinegar
1 tablespoon coconut oil
1 teaspoon basil, lightly chopped
2 tablespoons coconut, shredded (optional)

1. Preheat oven to 350°F.
2. Bring water to a boil, add lentils, and boil for 25 minutes, until lentils are firm but cooked. Drain and rinse under cold water.
3. Toast curry powder in the oven for 5 minutes.
4. In a sauté pan, heat 3 teaspoons of the sesame oil and cook onions until soft. Set aside.
5. In the same sauté pan, add remaining 1 teaspoon toasted sesame oil. Grill tofu until golden brown on both sides.
6. Add onions and tofu to the lentils, along with the curry, raisins, pears, vinegar, coconut oil, and basil.
7. Top with shredded coconut, if desired.
8. Serve immediately.

MAKES 4 SERVINGS.

EGGPLANT GARDEN DELIGHT

POWER 4

3–4 tablespoons olive oil
1 tablespoon sesame oil (optional)
1 clove garlic, peeled and chopped
1 long, thin eggplant, cut into
　strips
1–3 small baby summer squash,
　cut into 4 slices each to look like
　flowers
3–6 small–medium cherry
　tomatoes, halved
3–6 shiitake mushrooms, stems
　removed

1 or 2 green scallions
Spice Hunter Steak & Chop Grill
　& Broil seasoning*
3–6 asparagus, blanched
salt, to taste
pepper, to taste
cayenne, to taste
10 black olives, as garnish
　(optional)

1. In a large frying pan, heat olive oil over low heat and sauté garlic. (For a special taste, add a little toasted sesame oil, if desired.)
2. Place eggplant strips in pan and sauté until soft. Remove from pan, and set aside.
3. In the same frying pan, sauté squash, tomatoes, mushrooms, and scallions, and add seasoning while cooking. Cook until soft but do not overcook.
4. Combine all sautéed ingredients in a large dish and add asparagus.
5. Season with salt, pepper, and cayenne pepper to taste.
6. Arrange olives around edge of dish for garnish, if desired.
7. Serve immediately.

MAKES 2 SERVINGS.

Chef's Note: Spice Hunter Steak & Chop Grill & Broil seasoning contains garlic powder, onion powder, brown mustard powder, lemon peel powder, chili pepper powder, allspice powder, coriander powder, marjoram, and oregano.

EXOTIC CURRY CASSEROLE

POWER 2

2½ *tablespoons coconut oil*
½ *cup sunflower seeds*
1 *cup split peas, cooked*
⅓ *teaspoon curry*
¼ *teaspoon garlic, minced*
¼ *teaspoon salt*
¼ *teaspoon basil*
¼ *cup water*
½ *cup arugula, coarsely chopped*
1 *cup cauliflower, cut into bite-size pieces*
1 *cup brown rice, cooked*
½ *avocado, sliced, as garnish (optional)*

1. Preheat oven to 375°F. Lightly grease a 4-×-8 baking pan with some of the coconut oil.
2. In a blender, combine remaining coconut oil, sunflower seeds, split peas, curry, garlic, salt, basil, and water, and blend until smooth.
3. In the baking pan, combine arugula, cauliflower, and brown rice.
4. Add the blended seed and split pea mixture and bake for 15 minutes, covered.
5. Garnish with avocado slices, if desired.
6. Serve immediately.

MAKES 2 SERVINGS.

GARLIC TAHINI EGGPLANT

POWER 2

2½ tablespoons coconut oil
1 large eggplant (1½–1¾
  pounds)
4 cups cold water
5 tablespoons lemon juice, freshly
  squeezed
¼ teaspoon cayenne
¼ cup tahini
2 tablespoons fresh garlic, peeled
  and chopped
2 teaspoons lime juice

⅛ teaspoon dried fennel
4 tablespoons olive oil
½ cup red bell peppers, sliced
½ cup yellow bell peppers, sliced
1 cup vine-ripe tomatoes, diced
1 teaspoon sea salt
black pepper, freshly ground, to
  taste
2 tablespoons fresh dill, chopped
4 tablespoons agave or other
  sweetener

1. Preheat oven to 375°F. Lightly grease a 4-×-8 baking dish
   with coconut oil.
2. Using a toothpick or fork, pierce the eggplant several times,
   then place in the oiled baking dish. Bake until tender, about
   50 minutes.
3. Place eggplant in a large pot of cold water to cool quickly.
   Remove peel while still hot. Drain in colander until eggplant
   cools completely. Squeeze pulp to remove any bitter juices,
   and then purée the flesh.
4. In a blender or food processor, combine lemon juice,
   cayenne, tahini, garlic, lime juice, and fennel, and purée.
   Adjust quantities of seasonings for spicy or mild preferences.
   If necessary, thin with water, or thicken with ⅛–⅓ teaspoon
   flaxseed.
5. In a large bowl, combine puréed mixture, olive oil, bell
   peppers, tomatoes, salt, pepper, dill, and agave. Mix well and
   add puréed eggplant to the mixture.
6. Chill and serve cold.

MAKES 4 SERVINGS.

JAMAICAN CAKES

POWER 2

1 pound cassava
3 tablespoons olive oil
1 cup Vidalia onion, chopped
1 teaspoon Cajun seasoning
1 tablespoon sea salt
⅛ teaspoon black pepper, freshly ground
1 tablespoon egg substitute mixed with 1 tablespoon water
5 tablespoons agave or other sweetener
¼ cup pine nuts
olive oil for frying
carrots, shredded, as garnish (optional)

1. Peel cassava and grate it finely with grater or in food processor. Using cheesecloth, strain out as much juice as possible. (Raw cassava juice is not safe to cook with or to drink.)
2. In a large pan, heat 3 tablespoons olive oil over medium heat and sauté onion with Cajun seasoning, salt, and pepper.
3. In a bowl, combine egg substitute mixture and agave.
4. Add cassava flour and stir in sautéed onion and pine nuts.
5. In a heavy skillet, heat ¼ inch of oil on medium-high.
6. On a sheet of wax paper, mold the cassava pancakes and then transfer into skillet. Fry until both sides are toasty crisp.
7. Garnish with shredded carrots, if desired.
8. Serve warm.

MAKES 4 SERVINGS.

MARATHON MEAL

P O W E R   4

2 potatoes
4 tablespoons coconut oil
½ onion, peeled and diced
1 clove garlic, minced
¼ cup sun-dried tomatoes
¼ cup black olives
½ cup baked beans

1. Preheat oven to 350°F.
2. Bake the two potatoes for 1¼ hours.
3. In a medium-size pan, heat the oil over medium heat and sauté onion, garlic, sun-dried tomatoes, and black olives.
4. Add the baked beans and warm through.
5. Halve and scoop out the potatoes, and mix with the sautéed mixture. Then stuff the two halves of each baked potato with the sautéed mixture.
6. Serve immediately.

MAKES 1 SERVING.

MUSHROOM AND SWEET PEA SPAGHETTI

POWER 1

2 tablespoons olive oil
1 cup mushrooms, sliced
1 cup sweet peas
1 cup tomato, chopped
1/2 teaspoon basil
1/2 teaspoon salt
1/4 teaspoon oregano
2 cups whole grain spaghetti, cooked

1. In a large skillet, heat olive oil and sauté mushrooms, peas, and tomato with basil, salt, and oregano for 5 minutes.
2. Combine with spaghetti and toss gently.
3. Serve immediately.

MAKES 2 SERVINGS.

ORIENTAL GOLDEN RICE WITH TOFU

POWER 4

1³/4 cups water
2 teaspoons sea salt
1 cup brown jasmine basmati rice, uncooked
3 tablespoons olive oil
1 clove garlic, minced
1 scallion, chopped
1 tablespoon onion, minced
1¹/4 cups (6 ounces) coconut milk
2 curry leaves or bay leaves
1 14-ounce package firm tofu
¹/4 teaspoon ginger powder
¹/2 teaspoon turmeric
1 teaspoon parsley, minced
1 teaspoon toasted sesame seeds
several threads saffron
salt, to taste

1. In a saucepan, bring water and 1 teaspoon salt to a boil. Add rice, cover, and cook 17–20 minutes. When rice is done and water has been absorbed, spoon rice into a bowl.
2. In a large saucepan, heat oil over medium heat and sauté garlic, scallion, and onion, until onion is translucent. Transfer to another bowl.
3. In the same pan, over medium-high heat, combine coconut milk, curry or bay leaves, tofu, ginger, and turmeric.
4. Add the sautéed ingredients, parsley, sesame seeds, and saffron. As soon as the coconut milk begins to boil, add the cooked rice and bring the mixture to a boil.
5. Turn down the heat and simmer, uncovered, 12–15 minutes more.
6. Add salt to taste.
7. Serve warm.

MAKES 2 SERVINGS.

PIQUANT TEMPEH

POWER 8

2 tablespoons tamari

2 tablespoons white wine

1/2 pound tempeh, cut into 3/4-inch cubes

1 cup brown jasmine rice

2 1/2 cups water

1/2 cup plus 1 tablespoon arrowroot

1/4 cup dried shiitake mushrooms

boiling water (to cover mushrooms)

1/4 cup green and red peppers, cut into 1-inch cubes

1 tablespoon parsnips, sliced

1/2 cup snow peas or green beans

1 tomato, chopped

1/2 cup onion, cut into 1-inch cubes

1/8 cup bamboo shoots, thinly sliced

1/2 cup pineapple, drained, sliced, cut into bite-size pieces

1/4 cup pickled scallions, each halved

4 whole cloves garlic, peeled and crushed

4 thin slices fresh ginger, peeled

2 tablespoons olive oil for sautéing the tempeh

2 tablespoons agave or other sweetener

1/4 cup apple cider vinegar

sea salt, to taste

1/2 tablespoon light or golden miso sauce

1. In a bowl, mix the tamari and wine. Marinate tempeh 15 minutes.
2. In a medium-size saucepan, cook rice with 2 cups of the water over high heat. Once boiling, simmer, covered, for 40–45 minutes, until water is absorbed and rice is tender.
3. Place the arrowroot on a large sheet of waxed paper and dredge the tempeh in it, one piece at a time. Gently massage each piece to coat well. Throw away leftover arrowroot.
4. Place the mushrooms in a bowl and add enough boiling water to cover. Let stand 15 minutes, or until softened.
5. In a mixing bowl, combine the pepper cubes, parsnips, snow peas or green beans, tomato, onion, bamboo shoots, pineapple, scallions, garlic, and ginger.
6. Drain the mushrooms and squeeze to extract the moisture. Cut off and discard the stems and slice the mushrooms thinly. Add the mushrooms to the other vegetables and set aside.

7. In a wok, heat oil to the boiling point. Drop the dusted tempeh pieces, several at a time, into the oil. Cook 5–7 minutes, or until the tempeh is golden brown and crisp. Remove and drain on paper towels.

8. Drain off all except ⅛ cup of the oil, and add the mushroom and vegetable mixture to the wok. Cook, stirring, 4–5 minutes.

9. Meanwhile, in a saucepan, combine remaining ½ cup of water, agave, apple cider vinegar, and sea salt, and bring to a boil. Stir until smooth. Remove from heat and stir in light miso sauce.

10. Transfer the rice to a serving dish and place tempeh on top.

11. Add the miso sauce to the vegetables, and mix well.

12. Pour vegetables over the tempeh.

13. Serve immediately.

MAKES 2 SERVINGS.

POTATO STUFFED WITH SOYBEANS AND SHIITAKE MUSHROOMS

POWER 3

3 Idaho potatoes, baked, halved, with centers taken out and skins set
  aside
1 tablespoon fresh fennel, chopped
2 tablespoons fresh mint, chopped
1 cup soybeans, mashed
½ teaspoon paprika
½ teaspoon salt
½ teaspoon black pepper, freshly ground
1 cup shiitake mushrooms
2 cloves garlic
2–3 tablespoons olive oil
dash cayenne pepper

1. Preheat oven to 425°F.
2. In a large bowl, mash potatoes, fennel, mint, soybeans, paprika, salt, pepper, shiitake mushrooms, garlic, olive oil, and cayenne.
3. Stuff the mixture back into the potato skins. Bake for 10 minutes.
4. Serve immediately.

MAKES 2 SERVINGS.

RED BEANS WITH RICE

POWER 4

3 tablespoons olive oil
1 yellow onion, chopped
3 cloves garlic, peeled and mashed
1/2 red or yellow pepper, chopped
1 cup small red beans, cooked
2 cups boiling water
1 cup short-grain brown rice
3 tablespoons agave or other sweetener
1 tablespoon tamari sauce
pinch curry
1/2 teaspoon sea salt
pinch fresh ground pepper
hearts of palm, as garnish (optional)

1. In a pan, heat oil and sauté onion, garlic, and pepper until golden.
2. Place the sautéed ingredients into a saucepan, along with beans, water, rice, agave, tamari, curry, salt, and pepper. Simmer, covered, until rice is al dente, or to taste, about 35 minutes.
3. Garnish with hearts of palm, if desired.
4. Serve immediately.

MAKES 2 SERVINGS.

RIO RICE

P O W E R   1

2¹/₂ tablespoons toasted sesame oil
¹/₂ cup cauliflower florets, cut in bite-size pieces
2 tablespoons fresh parsley, chopped
2 tablespoons toasted sesame seeds
¹/₃ cup black beans, cooked
¹/₃ cup brown rice, cooked
¹/₂ teaspoon tamari
¹/₂ teaspoon salt
¹/₂ avocado, sliced, as garnish (optional)

1. Preheat the oven to 375°F. Lightly grease a 4-×-8 baking pan with toasted sesame oil.
2. Steam the cauliflower for about 5 minutes.
3. Combine cauliflower, parsley, sesame seeds, beans, rice, tamari, and salt. Mix well.
4. Transfer to baking pan and bake for 15 minutes.
5. Garnish with avocado slices, if desired.
6. Serve immediately.

MAKES 2 SERVINGS.

SEARED TOFU WITH ONIONS

POWER 6

2 tablespoons toasted sesame oil (equally divided)
½ teaspoon peppermint spice (divided)
1 cup red onion, sliced
1 cup white onion, sliced
7 cloves garlic, sliced
2 cups shiitake mushrooms, stemmed and sliced
8 marinated sun-dried tomatoes
6 leaves red lettuce
1 12-ounce package firm or extra-firm tofu
¼ cup mustard
2 teaspoons agave or other sweetener
7 black olives, as garnish (optional)
1 clump pickled ginger, as garnish (optional)
1 clump wasabi, as garnish (optional)

1. In a wok, heat 1 tablespoon sesame oil and ¼ teaspoon peppermint spice.
2. Sauté red onion, white onion, garlic, shiitake mushrooms, and sun-dried tomatoes.
3. Arrange on a plate over red lettuce leaves.
4. Cut tofu into 12 equal slices.
5. In a skillet, heat 1 tablespoon toasted sesame oil and ¼ teaspoon peppermint spice. Add tofu to pan and sear on both sides. Remove tofu from pan.
6. On a separate plate, brush mustard and agave on all sides of tofu, then top sautéed vegetables with tofu.
7. Garnish with black olives, pickled ginger, and wasabi in center, if desired.
8. Serve immediately.

MAKES 3 SERVINGS.

SEARED TOFU WITH ROASTED PEPPERS

POWER 2

4 tablespoons coconut oil
2 bell peppers, red and yellow
8 ounces tofu, sliced
¼ cup olive oil
1 tablespoon wine vinegar
sea salt, to taste
peppercorns, freshly ground, to taste
⅛ teaspoon Italian seasoning
1 teaspoon mustard
1 6-ounce jar of artichoke hearts, quartered
5 hearts of palm

1. Preheat oven to 350°F. Lightly grease baking sheet with 2 tablespoons coconut oil.
2. Bake whole peppers on oiled baking sheet 25–30 minutes, turning every 10 minutes. Remove from oven and allow to cool completely.
3. In a skillet, heat remaining coconut oil and sear each side of the tofu for 3 minutes, or until brown.
4. In a small bowl, whisk together olive oil, vinegar, salt, peppercorns, Italian seasoning, and mustard, and set aside.
5. Peel cooled peppers and cut them in half. Discard the seeds and cut peppers into strips. Toss peppers with artichoke hearts and hearts of palm.
6. Pour vinaigrette over vegetables.
7. Serve with seared tofu.

MAKES 4 SERVINGS.

SHIITAKE-STUFFED EGGPLANTS

POWER 2

2 small eggplants (or small zucchinis, with reduced cooking time)
2 tablespoons olive oil
1 yellow onion, chopped
1 cup fresh shiitake mushrooms, chopped
1 cup pomegranate juice
2/3 tablespoon maple syrup
pinch coarse sea salt
1/4 teaspoon black pepper, ground
1/4 teaspoon cumin
1/4 teaspoon cayenne
1/4 teaspoon fresh basil, crushed
3 small sprigs saffron
1 tablespoon water
1/4 cup cashews or hazelnuts, toasted
black pepper, to taste
salt, to taste
1 tablespoon cooking sherry
2 tablespoons sesame oil

1. Remove stems from eggplants and discard.
2. Gently roll each eggplant back and forth 4–5 times on counter to soften and facilitate removal of insides. Using a spoon, tunnel through the eggplant to within a quarter inch of each end. Remove and discard.
3. In a medium skillet, warm 2 tablespoons olive oil. Add onion, cover, and cook 5 minutes, or until onions are softened, not browned. Uncover and cook approximately 10 more minutes on medium heat, stirring occasionally.
4. Slowly increase heat to high and add mushrooms. Cook 2½ minutes, stirring.
5. Add pomegranate juice, maple syrup, coarse sea salt, black pepper, cumin, cayenne, basil, saffron, and 1 tablespoon water. Cook approximately 2 minutes, or until all water has cooked down.

6. Remove from heat and gently fold in cashews. Season to taste with black pepper, salt, and cooking sherry. Set mushroom-pomegranate stuffing aside.
7. Pat dry eggplant shells with paper towels. Pack each eggplant with mushroom-pomegranate stuffing using small spoon. Save extra stuffing.
8. In a skillet, heat sesame oil and sauté eggplant pulp until tender. Salt and pepper to taste.
9. Fill eggplant shells with sautéed eggplant. Top with extra mushroom-pomegranate stuffing.
10. Serve immediately.

MAKES 2 SERVINGS.

SOYBEANS WITH SESAME AND SWEET ONIONS

POWER 5

4 cups soybeans, fresh or frozen, cooked and cooled
4 cups mixed baby salad greens
4 scallions, sliced
1 cup shiitake mushrooms, destemmed and steamed
1 clove garlic, chopped
2 tablespoons flaxseed oil
2 tablespoons sesame seeds
2 tablespoons mustard
2 teaspoons lemon juice
1 teaspoon mint, lightly chopped
1 teaspoon salt

1. In a large bowl, combine soybeans, salad greens, scallions, shiitake mushrooms, garlic, flaxseed oil, sesame seeds, mustard, lemon juice, mint, and salt.
2. Mix well and serve chilled.

MAKES 4 SERVINGS.

SPICY PORTOBELLO MUSHROOMS
WITH GARLIC

POWER 2

1 teaspoon olive oil
2 tablespoons garlic, chopped
1 large portobello mushroom cap, cleaned and sliced
¼ teaspoon red pepper flakes
2 cups oregano sprouts or other spicy sprouts, washed
1 red pepper, deseeded and sliced
dash cayenne pepper

1. In a skillet, heat oil over medium heat and cook garlic, mushroom, and red pepper flakes until lightly brown, 10–15 minutes. Remove from heat.
2. Toss in sprouts, red pepper, and cayenne pepper, and mix well.
3. Serve immediately.

MAKES 2 SERVINGS.

STUFFED POTATOES WITH PINTO BEANS AND SOY CHEESE

POWER 3

2 Idaho potatoes, baked, halved, with centers taken out and skins set aside
2–3 tablespoons olive oil
2 tablespoons sweet onion, chopped
2 tablespoons fresh parsley, chopped
1 cup pinto beans
¼ teaspoon cayenne pepper
½ teaspoon paprika
1 teaspoon salt
½ teaspoon black pepper, freshly ground
1 cup soy cheese, shredded (optional)

1. Preheat oven to 425°F.
2. In a large bowl, mash potatoes, olive oil, onion, parsley, pinto beans, cayenne, paprika, salt, pepper, and soy cheese, if desired.
3. Stuff the mixture back into the potato skins and bake for 10 minutes.
4. Serve immediately.

MAKES 2 SERVINGS.

TEMPEH AND WHITE ASPARAGUS RAGOUT

POWER 6

1½ tablespoons olive oil
1 pound tempeh, cut into 1-inch cubes
1 Vidalia onion, ½ chopped and ½ sliced into rounds
1 scallion, chopped
2 cloves garlic, minced
1 tablespoon red bell pepper, minced
½ teaspoon sea salt
⅛ teaspoon black pepper, freshly ground
1 teaspoon ground cumin, divided
½ teaspoon curry powder
¼ teaspoon cayenne powder
¼ teaspoon turmeric
2 cups water
2 cups fresh white asparagus, cut into 2-inch pieces
1 ripe tomato, sliced into rounds
1 sprig watercress, chopped

1. In a large saucepan, heat the oil and add tempeh, chopped onion, scallion, garlic, and red bell pepper.
2. Sauté over low heat for 3–5 minutes, until onions are slightly clear.
3. Add salt, pepper, ½ teaspoon of the cumin, curry powder, cayenne powder, turmeric, and water. Bring to a boil and simmer over low heat for 45 minutes.
4. Add the white asparagus and cook for 15 minutes.
5. Add the sliced onion and tomato, and sprinkle the remaining ½ teaspoon of cumin and the watercress over the ragout sauce. Simmer for 15 minutes without stirring.
6. Serve hot.

MAKES 2 SERVINGS.

TEMPEH DINNER

POWER 5

2 tablespoons coconut oil
1 cup chickpeas, cooked
1 cup tempeh, cut into 1/2-inch cubes
1/2 cup broccoli florets, in bite-size pieces
1/2 cup soybean sprouts
1 tablespoon garlic, sliced
1 teaspoon fresh chives, chopped
1 teaspoon onion, minced
1 teaspoon salt

1. Preheat oven to 350°F. Lightly grease a 4-×-8 baking pan with coconut oil.
2. Combine chickpeas, tempeh, broccoli, sprouts, garlic, chives, onion, and salt, and mix well.
3. Transfer to baking pan and bake for 20 minutes.
4. Serve immediately.

MAKES 2 SERVINGS.

TEMPEH IN SHERRY SAUCE

POWER 5

1 pound tempeh or seitan, cut in chunks
3 tablespoons toasted sesame oil
¼ cup vegetable broth or water
¼ cup maple syrup
¼ cup dry sherry
pinch cayenne
3 tablespoons peanut oil
1 medium yellow onion, diced
6 cloves garlic, chopped
4 1-inch slices ginger
2 teaspoons spelt flour
1 bay leaf
1 tablespoon parsley, chopped
sea salt, to taste
black pepper, freshly ground, to taste
rice, cooked (optional)

1. Marinate the tempeh in sesame oil, broth, maple syrup, and sherry, with a pinch of cayenne.
2. In a large frying pan, heat peanut oil over medium heat, remove tempeh from marinade, set aside marinade, and sauté the tempeh for 2–3 minutes on both sides. Remove tempeh from the pan.
3. In the same pan, sauté the onion, garlic, and ginger in the oil until the onion is translucent.
4. Stir in the flour, then add the marinade and mix well. Add the bay leaf, parsley, and salt and pepper to taste, and simmer for 3–4 minutes.
5. Return the tempeh to the pan and cook, covered, over low heat for 3–4 minutes.
6. Serve over rice, if desired.

MAKES 2 SERVINGS.

TEMPEH MARINARA WITH RICE PENNE

POWER 3

12 ounces tempeh, cubed
1 cup yellow peppers, diced
1 cup white-capped mushrooms, sliced
4 cloves garlic, peeled and sliced
2 teaspoons soy sauce
1 teaspoon capers
2 teaspoons toasted sesame oil
1 cup marinara sauce (see recipe below)
½ pound rice penne
2 tablespoons olive oil

1. Add tempeh, peppers, mushrooms, garlic, soy sauce, capers, and sesame oil to marinara sauce and bring to a simmer.
2. Boil lightly salted water and cook penne until al dente.
3. Toss penne with marinara sauce and olive oil.
4. Serve immediately.

MAKES 3 SERVINGS.

MARINARA SAUCE*

POWER 3

1 tablespoon olive oil
1 medium onion, diced into ¹/₂-inch pieces
¹/₄ cup balsamic vinegar
4 cloves garlic, chopped
1 sprig thyme
1 bay leaf
1 28-ounce can of crushed tomatoes, or 3 large fresh tomatoes

1. In a thick-bottomed saucepan, heat oil and gently cook onion until soft. Add vinegar and reduce by half. Add garlic, thyme, bay leaf, and tomatoes. Simmer for 15 minutes.
2. Serve, or cool for later use.

Chef's Note: This is a basic marinara sauce. You may add olives, mushrooms, ground tempeh, and/or vegetables.

TOASTED SESAME TEMPEH

POWER 1

3 tablespoons macadamia nut oil
1 tablespoon toasted sesame seed oil
2 cups tempeh, cut into 1/2-inch pieces
2 tablespoons pine nuts
3 tablespoons sesame seeds
2 teaspoons fresh chives, minced
1 teaspoon tarragon
1 teaspoon salt
1 ounce water

1. Preheat oven to 350°F. Lightly grease baking sheet with macadamia nut oil.
2. In a heavy skillet, heat sesame oil and sauté tempeh for about 3 minutes.
3. In a blender or food processor, chop pine nuts until finely ground.
4. Mix nut meal with sesame seeds, chives, tarragon, salt, and 1 ounce of water.
5. Dip tempeh in the batter and place on baking sheet. Bake for 15 minutes.
6. Serve immediately.

MAKES 1 SERVING.

TOFU DUSTED WITH SPELT FLOUR

POWER 3

8 medium slices firm tofu
spelt flour for dusting
2 tablespoons toasted sesame oil
4 shiitake mushrooms

MARINADE:
   1 cup organic tamari
   black pepper
   1/2 teaspoon garlic powder
   1/2 teaspoon onion powder
   1/4 teaspoon brown mustard seeds
   2 tablespoons lemon peel
   dash chili pepper
   dash allspice
   dash coriander
   dash marjoram
   dash oregano
   dash cayenne

1. Whisk together tamari, black pepper, garlic powder, onion powder, brown mustard seeds, lemon peel, chili pepper, allspice, coriander, marjoram, oregano, and cayenne. Place tofu in marinade for 10 minutes, or marinate overnight for more flavor.
2. Dust marinated tofu with spelt flour.
3. In a skillet, heat 1 tablespoon sesame oil and sauté tofu, until slightly brown.
4. Sauté shiitake mushrooms in remaining 1 tablespoon of sesame oil, either together with tofu or separately.
5. Serve hot shiitake mushrooms over tofu or serve separately.

MAKES 4 SERVINGS.

TOFU, EGGPLANT, AND CHICKPEA STEW

POWER 4

1 tablespoon olive oil
1 pound firm tofu, sliced
1 medium onion, chopped (about 1/2 cup)
1 1/2 eggplants, cut crosswise into 1/2-inch slices
2 medium potatoes, peeled and sliced in 1/4-inch rounds
dash cayenne pepper
1/4 teaspoon saffron stamens or 1/4 teaspoon turmeric
1/2 teaspoon sea salt
1/3 cup dried chickpeas, soaked in water overnight and drained
1 1/2 cups water
2 medium cloves garlic
3/4 teaspoon cardamom, ground
1 tablespoon agave or other sweetener
1 tablespoon soy sauce
1 tablespoon sweet miso

1. In a large skillet, heat the oil over low heat and stir-fry tofu
   and onion for 5 minutes, until the onion becomes translucent.
2. Add the eggplants, potatoes, pepper, saffron, and salt, and
   continue to cook for an additional 5 minutes.
3. Add the chickpeas and water and bring to a boil. Lower heat,
   cover, and cook over low heat for 1 1/2 hours.
4. Crush the garlic and cardamom together in a mortar and stir
   into the stew.
5. Add the agave and soy sauce.
6. Simmer for 5 minutes and remove from heat.
7. Add miso and stir until well dissolved.*
8. Serve immediately.

MAKES 2 SERVINGS.

*Chef's Note: Never simmer miso; always add miso to a recipe after the cook-
ing process is done. There are several types of miso available; experiment and
use the one you like the best.

TOFU MARSALA

POWER 4

1 block firm tofu (or 2 packages)
spelt flour for dredging and thickening sauce
1⅓ tablespoons parsley, chopped
1½ tablespoons olive oil
garlic, minced, to taste
6 slices each portobello, maitake, and shiitake mushrooms
¾ cup Marsala wine, wine vinegar, or nonalcoholic balsamic vinegar
sea salt, to taste
½ teaspoon lemon pepper or black pepper, freshly ground

1. Dredge the tofu in spelt flour and ½ teaspoon of the parsley.
2. In a large skillet, warm the olive oil over medium heat. Add tofu and sauté on both sides, until golden. Remove tofu from pan.
3. In the same pan, sauté garlic and mushrooms for 5 minutes. Transfer to a bowl.
4. Pour wine or vinegar into the pan to deglaze. Reduce heat to low and stir 1 tablespoon of flour into the wine.
5. Return the tofu to the pan, turning to coat with the sauce.
6. Return mushrooms to the pan. Cook, covered, over low heat for 3 minutes.
7. Remove from pan, season with salt and pepper to taste, and sprinkle with remaining parsley.
8. Serve hot.

MAKES 6 SERVINGS.

TOFU-MUSHROOM RAGOUT
WITH ROASTED PINE NUTS AND PEARS

POWER 4

3 tablespoons olive oil
1 cup firm tofu, cubed
*1/2 cup shiitake mushrooms, stems removed, washed and halved**
1/2 cup crimini mushrooms, stems removed, washed and sliced
1/2 cup white mushrooms, stems removed, washed and sliced
1/2 cup maitake mushrooms, stems removed, washed and sliced
1/2 cup oyster mushrooms, stems removed, washed and halved
1 medium onion, diced
1/2 cup pear, diced
1/2 cup pine nuts
1 tablespoon tarragon, chopped
3 cloves garlic, crushed
2 tablespoons mustard seed oil
1 tablespoon soy sauce
black pepper

1. In a large skillet, heat oil and sauté tofu, mushrooms, and onion on low heat for about 10 minutes, or until all moisture has evaporated.
2. Add pear, pine nuts, tarragon, garlic, mustard seed oil, and soy sauce.
3. Season with pepper.
4. Serve hot or cold.

MAKES 2 SERVINGS.

Chef's Note: You may use any combination of the mushrooms listed or any other mushrooms.

TOFU PORTOBELLO BURGER

POWER 5

1 slice firm tofu or tempeh
¹/₂ cup tamari sauce
spelt flour for dusting
2 teaspoons olive oil
2 teaspoons toasted sesame oil
1 large portobello mushroom
1 clove garlic
1 onion, sliced very thin
1 large bun, pan-grilled, or 1–2 slices Ezekiel bread, toasted or pan-
*   heated with Earth Balance spread*
1 tomato slice
1 leaf romaine lettuce or salad vegetables
vegan mayonnaise
organic mustard sweetened with agave

1. Marinate tofu or tempeh in tamari sauce for 5 minutes, then dust with spelt flour.
2. In a skillet, heat olive oil and sesame oil and sauté mushroom and garlic for 5 minutes, or until tender.
3. Add tofu or tempeh and cook until golden brown. Onion can be added to the sauté or left raw, as desired.
4. Place each item on bun and dress with condiments to taste.
5. Serve immediately.

MAKES 1 SERVING.

TOFU WITH SESAME-PEANUT SAUCE

POWER 2

¹/₂ cup and ¹/₂ teaspoon sesame seeds
2 oranges, peeled, sliced, and seeded
1 tablespoon toasted sesame oil
1 cup oranges, juiced
¹/₄ teaspoon orange extract
dash soy sauce
1 12-ounce package firm tofu

1. In a large bowl, combine ¹/₂ cup sesame seeds, oranges, oil, orange juice, orange extract, and soy sauce, and mix well.
2. Place the tofu in the bowl and marinate for 1 hour in the refrigerator.
3. Remove the tofu from the marinade and broil about 8–10 minutes on each side.
4. Pour sesame-peanut sauce (**see recipe below**) over the tofu and sprinkle with remaining sesame seeds.
5. Serve with short-grain brown rice.

MAKES 3 SERVINGS.

SESAME-PEANUT SAUCE

POWER 3

1 cup water
¹/₃ cup tahini (raw)
¹/₃ cup peanut butter
¹/₆ cup tamari
2 tablespoons agave or other sweetener
1 inch ginger, grated
6 cloves garlic, minced
1 tablespoon toasted sesame oil (or hot sesame oil)
¹/₈ teaspoon cayenne, or to taste
¹/₈ teaspoon red chili flakes
pinch sea salt
pinch black pepper
2 tablespoons spelt flour

1. Whisk together water, tahini, peanut butter, tamari, agave, ginger, garlic, sesame oil, cayenne, red chili flakes, salt, and pepper.
2. Mix well and bring to a boil over medium heat.
3. Whisk in spelt flour to thicken. Reduce heat. Stir for 2–3 minutes.

TOFU WITH TOMATOES AND GARLIC

POWER 3

12 ounces firm tofu, cut into 2-inch cubes
1 tablespoon and 1 teaspoon garlic, chopped
1 cup tomatoes, diced into ¹/₂-inch pieces
¹/₄ cup organic red wine
1 tablespoon basil, chopped
1 tablespoon parsley, chopped
1 teaspoon soy sauce
1 tablespoon olive oil

1. Preheat oven to 350°F.
2. In a casserole dish, place tofu, garlic, tomatoes, and wine and bake, covered, for 15 minutes.
3. Remove tofu mixture from oven and add basil, parsley, soy sauce, and oil. Toss lightly.
4. Serve warm.

MAKES 2 SERVINGS.

WHOLE GRAIN SPAGHETTI WITH PESTO

POWER 3

1 clove elephant garlic, or 4 cloves regular garlic, pressed
1 scallion, chopped
1/2 teaspoon sea salt
1 1/4 cups fresh basil leaves
1/2 teaspoon dried fennel
9 tablespoons olive oil
1 ounce pine nuts (1/8 cup)
3/4 cup soy Parmesan cheese
1/2 teaspoon dried Italian seasoning
pinch cayenne pepper
12 ounces organic whole grain spaghetti
black pepper, freshly ground, to taste

1. Using a food processor, or mortar and pestle, mix the garlic, scallion, salt, basil, and fennel.
2. Add 3 tablespoons of olive oil, a little at a time. Slowly fold in the pine nuts, 1/4 cup of soy Parmesan cheese, Italian seasoning, and cayenne pepper.
3. Continue mixing with mortar and pestle or transfer to food processor and pulse for 1–2 minutes, or until the pesto sauce is a chunky consistency. Cover with 3 tablespoons of olive oil and refrigerate for 30 minutes before using.
4. Cook the spaghetti in plenty of lightly salted boiling water. Drain, saving a little of the cooking water to add to the pesto sauce.
5. In a large bowl, toss the spaghetti and the pesto and a little bit of the cooking water, along with the remaining 1/2 cup soy Parmesan and 3 tablespoons of olive oil. Sprinkle with black pepper.
6. Serve immediately.

MAKES 2 SERVINGS.

Chapter Ten

DESSERTS

ANYTIME GINGERBREAD

POWER 2

½ cup apple butter
½ cup agave or other sweetener
2 tablespoons coconut oil
2 tablespoons egg replacer
1 teaspoon orange extract
¼ cup rice milk
¾ cup spelt flour
1 teaspoon fresh ginger, grated or
  ground

1 teaspoon cinnamon, ground
1 teaspoon nutmeg, ground
1½ teaspoons baking powder
½ cup pecans, as garnish
  (optional)
orange slice, peeled, as garnish
  (optional)

1. Preheat oven to 325°F. Grease a standard loaf pan.
2. In a large bowl, combine the apple butter, agave, oil, egg replacer, orange extract, and rice milk.
3. In a separate bowl, mix the flour, ginger, cinnamon, nutmeg, and baking powder.

4. Fold flour mixture into apple butter mixture and stir until well combined.
5. Pour batter into the loaf pan and bake for 25–35 minutes. Gingerbread is done when the center of the cake springs back when touched or when a toothpick inserted into the center of the loaf comes out clean.
6. Garnish with pecans and orange, if desired.
7. Cool before serving.

MAKES 1 LOAF.

BAKED BANANAS AND RASPBERRIES

POWER 2

2–3 bananas, peeled
1 cup raspberries
2 tablespoons agave or other sweetener
1/8 teaspoon cinnamon
1/4 cup walnuts, chopped

1. Preheat oven to 350°F.
2. In a small casserole dish, place bananas with berries. Sprinkle agave, cinnamon, and walnuts on top.
3. Bake, covered, for 20 minutes.
4. Serve warm, alone or with frozen Rice Dream*

*Chef's Note: Rice Dream is a nondairy ice cream made from brown rice that can be purchased at most health food stores.

MAKES 2–3 SERVINGS.

BANANAS FLAMBÉ

POWER 1

3 ripe but not discolored bananas
1 tablespoon coconut oil
1 teaspoon Earth Balance buttery spread
1 tablespoon date sugar
2 tablespoons rice syrup or agave
½ teaspoon cinnamon
⅛ cup orange juice
1 teaspoon orange extract
1 teaspoon rum flavor extract
½ teaspoon orange zest
¼ cup currants
1 teaspoon vanilla extract
2 tablespoons dark rum
fresh mint leaves, as garnish (optional)

1. Peel bananas and slice in half lengthwise.
2. In a nonstick frying pan, heat coconut oil and Earth Balance over medium heat. Place bananas in pan, rounded side down. Cook approximately 5 minutes, turn bananas over, and cook another 5 minutes.
3. In a bowl, mix date sugar, rice syrup or agave, cinnamon, orange juice, orange and rum extracts, orange zest, currants, and vanilla. Pour over the bananas in the pan.
4. Cook 10 minutes over medium-low heat.
5. Remove the banana halves and arrange them on serving plates.
6. In the frying pan, heat the remaining juices until they begin to bubble. Remove from stove, add rum, and ignite sauce.
7. Pour flaming sauce over bananas with a flourish. Garnish with fresh mint leaves, if desire.
8. Serve immediately.

MAKES 3 SERVINGS.

CAROB-COATED NUTTY BANANA

POWER 1

1 cup carob chips
1/2 cup rice syrup
1/2 cup water
1 teaspoon vanilla extract
10 bananas, peeled, skewered lengthwise with sticks, and frozen
1 cup pecans, chopped

1. In a medium-size saucepan, combine the chips, syrup, water, and vanilla and cook over medium heat, stirring constantly, until the chips dissolve.
2. Remove melted mixture from heat.
3. Roll the frozen bananas in the carob mixture and then the nuts.
4. Place bananas on wax paper.
5. Freeze for 1 hour before serving.

MAKES 10 BANANAS.

CHERRY-BLUEBERRY FROZEN FRUIT

POWER 2

2 *bananas, peeled*
$^1/_2$ *cup agave or other sweetener*
$^1/_2$ *cup unsweetened coconut, shredded*
$^1/_2$ *cup cherries, pitted*
$^1/_2$ *cup blueberries*
$^1/_2$ *teaspoon cinnamon*

1. In a blender or food processor, combine all the ingredients and blend until smooth.
2. Pour into pop holders.
3. Freeze 1–2 hours before serving.

MAKES 12 POPS.

CLAIRE'S PEARS

1 tablespoon currants
dash cinnamon
2 pears, sliced
¹/₂ cup purified water
3 tablespoons agave or other sweetener
1 teaspoon orange extract
1 teaspoon almond extract
1 teaspoon lemon extract
1 teaspoon vanilla extract
1 tablespoon arrowroot liquid

1. In a medium-size bowl, mix together currants and cinnamon.
2. In a saucepan, add the pears, water, agave, orange, almond, lemon, and vanilla extracts, and heat until almost boiling.
3. Reduce heat and simmer for 20 minutes.
4. When pears are soft, add arrowroot liquid, and continue cooking over low heat until sauce thickens.
5. Remove from heat and pour mixture into a bowl. Stir in currants and cinnamon.
6. Serve immediately.

MAKES 2 SERVINGS.

DELICIOUS RASPBERRY TOFU PIE

POWER 1

1½ cups firm tofu
¼ cup agave
1½ teaspoons vanilla extract
pinch salt
egg substitute for 3 eggs
3 cups whole raspberries
9-inch unbaked, deep-dish springform pie shell (use The All-Purpose
  Pie Crust recipe, page 315)
whipped tofu cream or soy yogurt, for topping

1. Preheat oven to 400°F.
2. In a large mixing bowl, mash tofu until smooth, then stir in agave, vanilla, and salt.
3. Beat egg substitute and fold into the tofu mixture.
4. Wash the raspberries. Set aside 1 cup to use as topping. Gently mix the remaining 2 cups of raspberries into the tofu mixture.
5. Pour batter into the unbaked pie shell and bake for 10 minutes at 400°F, then lower oven to 325°F and bake for 35–40 minutes.
6. Cool for 1 hour.
7. Arrange the remaining raspberries on top of the cool pie, and top with tofu cream or soy yogurt.
8. Serve immediately.

MAKES ABOUT 8 SERVINGS.

DROP-DEAD-DELICIOUS BLUEBERRY PUDDING

POWER 2

2 cups blueberries*
2 cakes tofu, cut into 1/2-inch slices
3 tablespoons agave or other sweetener
1/2 teaspoon vanilla extract
dash cinnamon

1. Reserve small amount of blueberries for garnish.
2. In a blender, combine remaining blueberries, tofu, agave, vanilla, and cinnamon, and purée for 30–45 seconds.
3. Pour into 4 dessert cups and garnish with reserved blueberries.
4. Chill before serving.

MAKES 4 SERVINGS.

Chef's Note: This works well with almost any kind of fruit. Try substituting other types of berries, pears, oranges, or mangoes. Don't be afraid to be creative!

FROZEN GUAVA PEACH SUNDAE

POWER 1

2 guavas, peeled and frozen
4 peaches, pitted and frozen
1/2 cup fresh blueberries
3/4 cup raspberries
1/2 cup frozen strawberries, puréed

1. In a blender or food processor, blend the guavas until they have the consistency of ice cream.
2. Remove from blender and set aside.
3. Blend the peaches until they have the consistency of ice cream.
4. In a sundae glass, alternate layers of guava and peach.
5. Follow with a layer of blueberries and raspberries, and then top with the puréed strawberries.
6. Serve immediately.

MAKES 4–6 SERVINGS.

FRUIT MEDLEY WITH SAFFRON SAUCE

1 cup passion fruit, chopped or juiced
1¹/₂ cups pear juice
1 teaspoon saffron threads
¹/₂ cup strawberries, halved
¹/₄ cup mango, sliced
¹/₄ cup papaya, sliced
¹/₄ cup red grapes, pitted
1 cup vanilla Rice Dream*

1. In a medium-size saucepan, combine the passion fruit, pear juice, and saffron, and bring to a simmer over medium heat.
2. Remove from heat and toss in the remaining fruit.
3. Serve warm over Rice Dream.

MAKES 2 SERVINGS.

*Chef's Note: Rice Dream is a nondairy ice cream made from brown rice that can be purchased at most health food stores.

GERMAN CHOCOLATY CAKE

POWER 1

2 tablespoons macadamia nut oil
flour for dusting pan
1³/₄ cup Florida Crystals
¹/₃ cup peanut oil
1 cup soymilk
¹/₂ cup almond slivers
¹/₃ cup fresh coconut, flaked or grated
3 ounces nutritious or dark chocolate (dark is ideal)
¹/₂ cup olive oil
1 cup egg substitute
pinch cinnamon
1 teaspoon vanilla extract
1 teaspoon almond extract
¹/₂ cup brown rice flour
¹/₂ cup buckwheat flour
³/₄ teaspoon baking soda
pinch sea salt

1. Preheat oven to 350°F. Oil an 8-inch-square baking pan with macadamia nut oil and dust with flour.
2. In a heavy saucepan, combine ¾ cup Florida Crystals, peanut oil, and soymilk over medium-low heat for 10 minutes, stirring frequently.
3. Remove from heat, and add almond slivers and coconut. Distribute evenly over bottom of prepared pan. Set aside.
4. In the top of a double boiler, melt nutritious or dark chocolate over medium-high heat, stirring until liquefied. Set aside.
5. In a large mixing bowl, cream remaining 1 cup Florida Crystals and olive oil until fluffy.
6. Beat in egg substitute and cinnamon.
7. Stir in melted chocolate and vanilla and almond extracts.
8. In a separate bowl, combine flours, baking soda, and salt.
9. Fold flour mixture into batter and blend.

10. Layer batter over almond and coconut mixture in cake pan, and bake until toothpick inserted in center of cake comes out clean, about 60–75 minutes. Do not overcook. Do not open oven before 35 minutes—cake may fall.

11. Remove from oven and cool on a wire rack for 10–15 minutes. Loosen cake by running a knife around the rim of the pan.

12. Turn cake upside down over serving plate, and lift pan off. Allow to cool completely before frosting with mocha frosting (**see recipe below**).

MAKES 4 SERVINGS.

MOCHA FROSTING

¹/₄ cup rice syrup
1 teaspoon almond extract
¹/₃ cup tahini
1 teaspoon cinnamon, ground
3 tablespoons pure maple syrup
1 tablespoon Caffix or coffee substitute
1 teaspoon carob powder

1. In a small saucepan, combine the rice syrup, almond extract, tahini, cinnamon, maple syrup, Caffix, and carob powder, and cook over medium heat for 5 minutes, stirring constantly.

2. Allow to cool before using.

MAKES ¹/₂–³/₄ CUP.

GORGEOUS STRAWBERRY YOGURT PIE

POWER 1

$1^1/2$ *cups plain soy yogurt*
egg substitute for 3 eggs, beaten
$^1/4$ *cup unsalted nondairy butter, melted*
$^1/4$ *cup agave*
$1^1/2$ *teaspoon vanilla extract*
pinch salt
$2^1/2$–*3 cups whole strawberries, washed and hulled*
1 The All-Purpose Pie Crust (see recipe, page 315)
tofu cream or soy yogurt, as topping

1. Preheat oven to 400° F.
2. In a mixing bowl, combine soy yogurt, egg substitute, nondairy butter, agave, vanilla, and salt. Beat until very smooth.
3. Separate the soft, ripe strawberries from the firmer ones. You will need about 2 cups of soft strawberries and 1 cup of firm ones. Slice the firm berries in half and reserve.
4. Mix the soft strawberries with the yogurt mixture.
5. Pour this mixture into the unbaked pie shell and bake at 400°F for 10 minutes, then lower oven temperature to 325°F and continue baking for 35–40 minutes.
6. Remove from the oven and allow pie to cool for 1 hour.
7. Arrange the sliced, firm strawberries on top of the cool pie. Top with tofu cream or soy yogurt.
8. Serve immediately.

MAKES ABOUT 8 SERVINGS.

KIWI KANTEN

POWER 2

1/2 cup kiwi, chopped
1/2 cup apple, chopped
1/2 orange, diced and seeded
1 banana, sliced
2 cups nectarine juice
4 tablespoons maple syrup
3 tablespoons agave or other sweetener
8–10 teaspoons agar-agar
1 tablespoon arrowroot
1 teaspoon nutmeg, ground
1/2 teaspoon vanilla extract

1. In a blender, purée the kiwi, apple, orange, and banana until smooth.
2. Transfer the fruit blend into a medium-size saucepan and bring to a boil.
3. Stir in the nectarine juice, maple syrup, agave, agar-agar, arrowroot, nutmeg, and vanilla, reduce heat to medium, and cook for 5 minutes.
4. Remove from heat and pour into a mold.
5. Chill until firm, 2–3 hours, before serving.

MAKES 2 SERVINGS.

MANGO PECAN MAPLE CUSTARD

POWER 1

3 cups silken tofu
1/2 cup mango
4 tablespoons apple juice
4 tablespoons vanilla extract
4 1/2 teaspoons almond extract
1/4 cup pecans

1. In a blender or food processor, combine the tofu, mango, apple juice, and vanilla and almond extracts, and blend until smooth.
2. Top with pecans.
3. Serve chilled.

MAKES 4 SERVINGS.

NUTTY CAROB-PECAN FUDGE

POWER 1

1 cup soymilk or rice milk
1 cup carob chips
3/4 cup carob powder
3/4 cup peanut butter
1/2 cup agave or other sweetener
1/2 cup carob syrup
1 teaspoon vanilla extract
1 cup unsweetened coconut
1 cup pecans, halved

1. In a large bowl, mix the soymilk or rice milk, carob chips, carob powder, peanut butter, agave, carob syrup, and vanilla extract.
2. Form mixture into patties. Roll each patty in coconut and top with a pecan half.
3. Serve immediately.

MAKES 15–20 PATTIES.

ORANGE PECAN PIE

POWER 1

2 cups agave or other sweetener
1/2 teaspoon orange rind, grated
1/2 teaspoon orange extract
3 cups pecans
1 The All-Purpose Pie Crust (see recipe, page 315)

1. Preheat oven to 350°F.
2. In a medium-size bowl, combine the agave, orange rind, and orange extract, and mix well.
3. Distribute the pecans evenly in the bottom of the pie crust.
4. Pour the syrup mixture over the pecans and smooth it out evenly.
5. Bake for 30 minutes and allow to cool for 1 hour.
6. Serve chilled, with nondairy vanilla ice cream, if desired.

MAKES ONE 9-INCH PIE.

PAPAYA PUDDING POPS

POWER 1

1 cup papaya, peeled and sliced
1/4 cup rice milk or soymilk
2 tablespoons agave or other sweetener
1/8 teaspoon cinnamon

1. In a blender, combine papaya, rice milk or soymilk, agave, and cinnamon, and blend until smooth.
2. Pour into pop holders.
3. Freeze 1–2 hours before serving.

MAKES 8 POPS.

RASPBERRY SAUCE
OVER POACHED PEACHES

4 peaches, peeled and halved
2 cups apple juice
1 teaspoon lemon extract
2 cups raspberries, fresh or frozen
¾ cup maple sugar
4 fresh mint leaves, as garnish (optional)

1. In a large saucepan, bring the peaches, apple juice, and lemon extract to a boil, reduce heat to low, and cook, covered, for 5 minutes. Remove from heat and drain.
2. In a separate saucepan, combine the raspberries and sugar. Bring to a simmer and let cook for 2 minutes. Remove from heat and serve over the drained peaches.
3. Garnish with the mint leaves, if desired.
4. Serve immediately. Excellent with nondairy vanilla ice cream such as Rice Dream.*

MAKES 2 SERVINGS.

*Chef's Note: Rice Dream is a nondairy ice cream made from brown rice that can be purchased at most health food stores.

SPANISH COCONUT CUSTARD

POWER 1

egg substitute for 2 egg yolks
2/3 cup soymilk
2 tablespoons arrowroot
1 tablespoon coconut milk
2 teaspoons vanilla extract
1/4 cup unsweetened coconut, shredded

1. In a medium-size saucepan, combine the egg substitute, soymilk, arrowroot, coconut milk, and vanilla.
2. Whisk well and cook over low heat, stirring constantly, until mixture thickens.
3. Remove from heat and stir in the coconut.
4. Chill before serving.

MAKES 2 SERVINGS.

SUMPTUOUS BANANA CREAM PIE

POWER 2

3 tablespoons agave or other sweetener
¹/₄ teaspoon salt
4 tablespoons arrowroot
2 cups soymilk or rice milk
egg substitute for 2 eggs, well beaten
¹/₄ teaspoon lemon extract
3 bananas, peeled and sliced in rounds
1 prebaked The All-Purpose Pie Crust (see recipe, page 315)

1. In a heavy saucepan, stir together the agave, salt, and arrowroot over low heat.
2. Add the rice milk or soymilk, stirring constantly, until the mixture thickens.
3. Remove from heat and add the egg substitute, continuing to stir.
4. Return to the stove and, stirring constantly, cook for about 8 minutes, until the mixture thickens.
5. Remove from heat and stir in lemon extract.
6. Place a layer of half of the sliced bananas over the bottom of the pie crust. Pour half of the cream filling over the bananas. Follow with another layer of bananas, then the other half of the cream filling.
7. Allow pie to cool completely before placing in the refrigerator.
8. Serve chilled.

MAKES ABOUT 8 SERVINGS.

SWEET CARROT HALVAH

POWER 3

3 cups carrots, shredded
¹/₂ cup (1 stick) nondairy butter (like Earth Balance)
2–4 tablespoons cottage-style nondairy cheese
4 cups soymilk
¹/₂ cup tahini
¹/₂ cup raisins
¹/₂ cup almonds, chopped
¹/₂ cup pistachio nuts, finely chopped
¹/₂ cup cashews, finely chopped
¹/₂ cup walnuts, finely chopped
¹/₄ cup maple sugar
5 teaspoons cardamom, ground

1. In a large saucepan over medium heat, sauté the carrots in the nondairy butter until they turn red, approximately 5–7 minutes.
2. Stir in the cheese, soymilk, and tahini, and cook an additional 5–10 minutes.
3. In a separate bowl, mix together the raisins, nuts, maple sugar, and cardamom, and sprinkle over the carrot mixture.
4. Serve hot or cold.

MAKES 6 SERVINGS.

SWEET PUMPKIN FLAN

POWER 1

2 tablespoon hazelnut or canola oil
3 tablespoons brown rice syrup
1 cup acorn squash or pumpkin, cooked or canned
1/4 cup agave or other sweetener
1/4 cup rice milk
2 tablespoons arrowroot
3 teaspoons vanilla extract
1 teaspoon almond extract
1/2 teaspoon fennel
1/2 teaspoon cinnamon
pinch salt
toasted coconut and slivered almonds for topping

1. Preheat oven to 350°F. Oil a small baking dish and spread brown rice syrup evenly on bottom.
2. In a small bowl, combine squash or pumpkin, agave, rice milk, arrowroot, vanilla extract, almond extract, fennel, cinnamon, and salt, and mix until smooth.
3. Pour mixture over brown rice syrup and bake for 45 minutes.
4. Top with coconut and almonds.
5. Refrigerate until well chilled before serving.

MAKES 2 SERVINGS.

SWEET RASPBERRY-BLUEBERRY CRUMBLE

POWER 1

1/2 cup rice flour
1/4 cup spelt flour
1 tablespoon arrowroot
3/4 cup Florida Crystals
3 ounces Earth Balance buttery spread, melted
1/2 cup blueberries, fresh or frozen
1/2 cup raspberries, fresh or frozen
2 teaspoons lemon juice, freshly squeezed
1/4 cup agave or other sweetener
1/4 teaspoon cinnamon
*2 dollops whipped soy cream for topping**

1. Preheat oven to 300°F.
2. In a large bowl, mix flours, arrowroot, and Florida Crystals.
3. Add melted buttery spread and mix with pastry blender until mixture resembles bread crumbs.
4. In a soufflé dish, combine blueberries and raspberries and sprinkle with lemon juice, agave, and cinnamon.
5. Cover berries evenly with the crumble topping, pressing down gently.
6. Bake for 17–23 minutes, or until topping is golden-brown.
7. Top with whipped soy cream sweetened with agave and berries.
8. Serve hot or cold.

MAKES 2 SERVINGS.

Chef's Note: For a special treat, drizzle with melted dark chocolate or heated raspberry jam.

SWEET TOFU WHIPPED CREAM

POWER 1

1 8-ounce package silken tofu
¼ cup pure maple syrup
1 teaspoon lemon extract
1 teaspoon egg replacer
½ teaspoon vanilla extract

1. Whip or blend tofu, maple syrup, lemon extract, egg replacer, and vanilla extract for 1 minute, or until firm.
2. Serve chilled.

MAKES 4 SERVINGS.

SWEET TREAT TAHINI COOKIES

1 cup tahini
1/2 cup (1 stick) nondairy butter (like Earth Balance)
1 cup agave or other sweetener
1 1/2 teaspoons almond extract
4 cups spelt flour
1 teaspoon baking powder
1 1/2 cups unsweetened coconut, shredded
1/2 cup sesame seeds

1. Preheat oven to 375°F. Grease a flat cookie sheet.
2. In a large bowl, combine the tahini, nondairy butter, agave, and almond extract, and blend well.
3. In a separate bowl, combine the flour and baking powder. Fold into the batter and stir well.
4. Mix in the coconut and sesame seeds.
5. Roll the dough into balls and press onto greased cookie sheet. Bake for 25–30 minutes, until light brown.
6. Cool before serving.

MAKES ABOUT 30 LARGE COOKIES.

SWEETIES' SWEET POTATO PIE

POWER 2

2 tablespoons canola oil
²/₃ cup firmly packed date sugar or maple syrup
2 tablespoons agave or other sweetener
1¹/₂ cups sweet potatoes, boiled and mashed (2 large or 3 medium)
¹/₄ cup applesauce
egg substitute equivalent to 1 egg
¹/₄ cup French vanilla soy creamer
1¹/₂ teaspoons vanilla extract
¹/₂ teaspoon nutmeg
¹/₄ teaspoon cinnamon
¹/₄ teaspoon sea salt
¹/₈ teaspoon ginger
¹/₈ teaspoon lemon concentrate
1 The All-Purpose Pie Crust (see recipe, page 315)
almonds or shredded coconut for topping

1. Preheat oven to 425°F.
2. In a large bowl, blend oil, date sugar or maple syrup, and agave until light and fluffy.
3. Mix in sweet potatoes and applesauce.
4. Add egg substitute and beat vigorously.
5. Add creamer, vanilla, nutmeg, cinnamon, sea salt, ginger, and lemon concentrate, and continue beating mixture to a smooth, creamy consistency.
6. Pour the mixture into the pie crust and bake for 10 minutes at 425°F.
7. Lower oven temperature to 325°F and bake for an additional 35 minutes, or until a knife inserted into the center of the pie comes out clean.
8. Cool thoroughly and sprinkle with almonds or shredded coconut before serving.

MAKES 4–6 SERVINGS.

THE ALL-PURPOSE PIE CRUST

POWER 1

2 cups whole spelt flour, sifted, plus 1/4 cup for rolling out crust
1/8 teaspoon nutmeg, ground
dash salt
1/2 cup cold rice milk or soymilk
1/2 cup oat flour
1/2 cup coconut oil

1. Preheat oven to 350°F.
2. In a medium-size bowl, combine the whole spelt flour, nutmeg, and salt.
3. Add rice milk or soymilk, oat flour, and coconut oil and stir until moistened throughout. (Add the cold milk by the tablespoon until the dough is of even consistency.)
4. Roll the dough into two balls and chill dough as for conventional pie crust.
5. Flour a smooth surface and a rolling pin with oat flour. Then roll the dough out from the center until it is 1/2 inch larger than the pie plate. (You can measure by placing the plate on top of the rolled dough.)
6. Transfer the crust to the pie plate by gently sliding a floured spatula underneath the crust, toward its center. Do this around the entire area of the crust, then fold it over on itself and slide it into the pie plate, and unfold.
7. Repeat the procedure with the second ball of dough, to use for a top crust.
8. Bake pie crust for 15 minutes, or until light brown, when the recipe calls for a baked shell. Do not overcook or crust will become too chewy.

MAKES TWO 9-INCH CRUSTS.

SECTION 3

Chapter   Eleven

TWO-WEEK MEAL PLAN

These menus show you just how easy it is to incorporate the Power Foods into your daily eating habits for a diet that is tasty, varied, and most beneficial for your good health. Each dish is followed by its Power Food designation so you can see at a glance how easy it is to enjoy the benefits of the Power Foods in your daily eating plan. As you become familiar with all the recipes in this book, you can become as creative as you like, mixing and matching dishes for your particular preferences.

Week One

DAY 1

Daily Total of Power Foods: 24

Breakfast
   Amish Amaranth (P1)

Snack
  Sweet Onion-Cheddar Delight on Spelt Crackers (P2)
Lunch
  Acorn Squash Bake (P3)
  Wilted Arugula with Oyster Mushrooms and Soy Parmesan (P2)
Dinner
  Soup: Anytime Gazpacho (P6)
  Salad: Potato–Green Bean Salad (P2)
  Entrée: Tofu Portobello Burger (P5)
  Dessert: Cherry-Blueberry Frozen Fruit (P2)
Evening Juice
  Healthy Milk Shake (P1)

DAY 2

Daily Total of Power Foods: 22

Breakfast
  Berry Bulgur (P4)
Snack
  Hummus to Mummus on Pita Toast (P3)
Lunch
  Exotic Curry Casserole (P2)
  Sautéed Kale with Shiitake Mushrooms (P2)
Dinner
  Soup: Cream of Cauliflower-Broccoli Soup (P2)
  Salad: Endive with Basil and Sprouts (P3)
  Entrée: Cambodian Soba Peanut Noodles (P4)
  Dessert: Mango Pecan Maple Custard (P1)
Evening Juice
  Red and Yellow Pepper Apple Juice (P1)

DAY 3

Daily Total of Power Foods: 16

Breakfast
　　Carob-Blueberry Quinoa (P3)
Snack
　　Nutty Soy Cheese Spread on Celery Sticks (P1)
Lunch
　　Cajun Tofu (P1)
　　Kombu Seaweed with Toasted Sesame (P3)
Dinner
　　Soup: Mediterranean White Bean Soup (P3)
　　Salad: Coleslaw with Fresh Fennel (P1)
　　Entrée: Savory Butternut Squash (0)
　　Dessert: Sweeties' Sweet Potato Pie (P2)
Evening Juice
　　Cherry-Jammin' Juice (P2)

DAY 4

Daily Total of Power Foods: 21

Breakfast
　　Hawaiian Coconut Buckwheat Cereal (P2)
Snack
　　Fresh Herbal Spread on Rice Crackers (P4)
Lunch
　　Spicy Portobello Mushrooms with Garlic (P2)
　　New Southern Greens (P2)
Dinner
　　Soup: Onion Shiitake Soup (P3)
　　Salad: Yukon Gold Potato Salad (P1)
　　Entrée: Eggplant Garden Delight (P4)
　　Dessert: Anytime Gingerbread (P2)
Evening Juice
　　Fruity Spritzer (P1)

DAY 5

Daily Total of Power Foods: 24

Breakfast
   It's Nice with Rice (P1)
Snack
   Sweet Potato–Broccoli Cream Dip on Carrot Sticks (P2)
Lunch
   Black & Green Olive Ratatouille (P3)
   Swiss Chard and Red Potatoes (P5)
Dinner
   Soup: Papaya Yam Soup (P0)
   Salad: Sesame Bean Salad (P3)
   Entrée: Chili con Tempeh (P7)
   Dessert: Baked Bananas and Raspberries (P2)
Evening Juice
   Hawaiian Juice (P1)

DAY 6

Daily Total of Power Foods: 21

Breakfast
   Magic Millet (P2)
Snack
   Tropical Spicy Guacamole on Corn Chips (P2)
Lunch
   Tempeh in Sherry Sauce (P5)
   Sticky Black Sweet Rice on Mango (P1)
Dinner
   Soup: Spicy Gingery Lima Bean Soup (P3)
   Salad: Romaine Hearts Sprout Salad (P3)
   Entrée: Tofu with Sesame-Peanut Sauce (P2)
   Dessert: Orange Pecan Pie (P1)
Evening Juice
   Berry Citrus Slush (P2)

DAY 7

Daily Total of Power Foods: 24

Breakfast
Orange-Glazed Apples with Quinoa (P3)
Snack
Spicy Eggplant Spread on Pita Chips (P4)
Lunch
Baby Lima Bean and Mushroom Sauté (P3)
China Sea Seaweed Salad (P3)
Dinner
Soup: Tart Cherry and Raspberry Soup (P1)
Salad: African Millet Salad (P4)
Entrée: Tofu Marsala (P4)
Dessert: Spanish Coconut Custard (P1)
Evening Juice
Chlorophyll for Life (P1)

Week Two

DAY 8

Daily Total of Power Foods: 28

Breakfast
Apple French Toast with Banana Sauce (P2)
Snack
Badass Bean Dip on Tortilla Chips (P3)
Lunch
Algerian Spicy Tofu Chili (P7)
Broccoli Wild Rice (P2)
Dinner
Soup: Miso Tofu Vegetable Soup (P7)
Salad: Bangkok Salad (P4)
Entrée: Garlic Tahini Eggplant (P2)

Dessert: Nutty Carob-Pecan Fudge (P1)
Evening Juice
Cantaloupe and Sweet Potato Juice (P0)

DAY 9

Daily Total of Power Foods: 25

Breakfast
Blueberry Spelt Pancakes (P3)
Snack
Spicy Raw Thai Roll-Ups (P1)
Lunch
Soybeans with Sesame and Sweet Onions (P5)
Braised Endive (P2)
Dinner
Soup: Oriental Mushroom Soup (P5)
Salad: Pear Beet Salad (P2)
Entrée: Tofu Dusted with Spelt Flour (P3)
Dessert: Kiwi Kanten (P2)
Evening Juice
Lush Pecan Shake (P2)

DAY 10

Daily Total of Power Foods: 21

Breakfast
South Pacific Rice Cereal (P1)
Snack
Gourmet Spicy Tofu Dip on Pita Triangles (P2)
Lunch
Toasted Sesame Tempeh (P1)
Healthy Hijiki (P2)
Dinner
Soup: Kicking Miso Soup (P6)

Salad: Watercress, Orange, and Endive Salad (P6)
Entrée: Mushroom and Sweat Pea Spaghetti (P1)
Dessert: Sweet Treat Tahini Cookies (P0)
Evening Juice
Peppermint Shake (P2)

DAY 11

Daily Total of Power Foods: 27

Breakfast
Millet Almond Cinnamon (P2)
Snack
Nutty Soy Cheese Spread on Carrot Sticks (P1)
Lunch
Seared Tofu with Onions (P6)
Roasted Root Vegetables (P4)
Dinner
Soup: Creamy Tomato-Potato Soup (P4)
Salad: Power-Filled Waldorf Salad (P1)
Entrée: Tempeh and White Asparagus Ragout (P6)
Dessert: Papaya Pudding Pops (P1)
Evening Juice
Celery Sip (P2)

DAY 12

Daily Total of Power Foods: 20

Breakfast
Creamy Carob-Coconut Amaranth (P2)
Snack
Sweet Onion-Cheddar Delight on Celery Sticks (P2)
Lunch
Tempeh Dinner (P5)
Mixed Mushrooms Salad with Hearts of Palm (P3)

Dinner
  Soup: Sweet and Sour Soup (P4)
  Salad: Tofu and Bean Salad (P2)
  Entrée: Aromatic Thai Rice (P1)
  Dessert: Claire's Pears (P0)
Evening Juice
  Hot Potato Cool Tomato (P1)

DAY 13

Daily Total of Power Foods: 25

Breakfast
  Cocoa Kasha with Blueberries (P3)
Snack
  Tangy Tomato Salsa with Corn Chips (P3)
Lunch
  Jamaican Cakes (P2)
  Succulent Cranberry Sauce (P0)
Dinner
  Soup: Curried Carrot Soup (P6)
  Salad: Have-a-Lotta Insalata (P4)
  Entrée: Stuffed Potatoes with Pinto Beans and Soy Cheese (P3)
  Dessert: Sweeties' Sweet Potato Pie (P2)
Evening Juice
  Almond Shake (P2)

DAY 14

Daily Total of Power Foods: 21

Breakfast
  Sweet Spice Quinoa (P1)
Snack
  Tropical Spicy Guacamole on Pita Chips (P2)

Lunch
>Tofu with Tomatoes and Garlic (P3)
>Whole Grain Spaghetti with Pesto (P3)

Dinner
>**Soup:** Parsnip-Potato Soup (P2)
>**Salad:** Indian Arugula Salad (P3)
>**Entrée:** Asian Rice Noodles (P4)
>**Dessert:** German Chocolaty Cake (P1)

Evening Juice
>A Taste of Eden (P2)